CREATE & MAINTAIN YOUR

Smallholding

LIZ WRIGHT

Publisher and Creative Director: Nick Wells
Senior Project Editor: Catherine Taylor
Art Director: Mike Spender
Layout Design: Jane Ashley
Digital Design & Production: Chris Herbert
Copy Editor: Anna Groves
Proofreader: Dawn Laker
Indexer: Helen Snaith

Also thanks to: Carolyn Bingley, Magda Pszuk, Frances Bodiam.

Special thanks to Henrietta Breitmayer, Oliver Didier'serre, Grace
Cooper and Mick Knight who help me play with ponies.

FLAME TREE PUBLISHING

6 Melbray Mews, Fulham,
London SW6 3NS, United Kingdom
www.flametreepublishing.com

First published 2018

© 2018 Flame Tree Publishing Ltd

22 21 20 19 18
10 9 8 7 6 5 4 3 2 1

ISBN 978-1-78664-772-6

A CIP record for this book is available from the British Library upon request.

Many thanks to the following for kindly supplying images – courtesy and ©: **Liz Wright:** 70, 71, 75, 169t, 173b; **Timber Flair:** 113t; **Rupert Stephenson:** 117b, 126tl, 126b, 127b, 128b; **Mick Corrigan:** 122t, 124tr, 124tc, 124tl, 125b, 162t; Omlet (www.omlet.co.uk): 157b, 158, 160t, 160t; **Flyte So Fancy Ltd** (www. flytesofancy.co.uk): 160b; **IAE:** 173t, 180; **Grandpa's Feeders:** 223b. Images of book covers © Flame Tree Publishing Ltd. Other pictures courtesy of **Shutterstock** and ©: Manaraga 1 & 3; Have a nice day Photo 4b & 33; kropic1 4t & 17; brackish_nz 5b & 109; Cherries 5t & 61; Africa Studio 6b & 185; Nick Beer 6t & 151; Magdanatka 7t & 211; StockLite 7b & 229; unknown various 8t, 41b, 100t, 104b, 106, 122b, 146t, 149 & 150, 153, 156t & 210, 160r, 219t, 243t, 249b mavo 8b, 25, 30, 227; wavebreakmedia 9, 115b, 193; Dmitry Lampy 10t & 60; Juhku 10bl; Zaretskaya Svetlana 11; Christian Jung 12; sirtravelalot 13, 20, 243b; angelakatharina 14; Vasilyeva Larisa 15 & 32, 186t, 207t; Angorius 16; eldar nurkovic 18; Milosz_G 19, 137; alexmak7 21; Brian Stewart-Coxon 22t; Monkey Business Images 22b, 57, 110, 188; O.C Ritz 23; Anna Nikonorova 24b; Olga Tropinina 24t & 118t; Ivonne Wierink 26, 146b; Olesia Agudova 27b & 184, 83t; Take Photo 27t; casanisa 28b, 196, 245; Kkris 28t; Montira 29; Lubawko 31b, 47, 62 & 248t, 64, 247; wutzkohphoto 31t, 48; goodluz 34, 80; SpeedKingz 35; Nadezda Razvodovska 36; metriognome 37; Ttphoto 38; Anna ART 39; Iladyjane 40t; nortivision 40b; Ann Louise Hagevi 41t; Ellen Morgan 42b; Tahoo 42t; grahamspics 43; AnnaElizabeth photography 44; Chukov 45; Oksana Kuzmina 46; Budimir Jevtic 50, 172t, 216; Bartosz Ostrowski 51b; Netkoff 51t; kittirat roekburi 52; Alexander_P 53b; Peter Turner Photography 53t, 54; Heath Johnson 55; antony cullup 56; Iuliia Bondarenko 58; Flipser 59; EMJAY SMITH 63bc; Fabio Lamanna 63tr; Madlen 63bl; MemoPlus 63br; Oleg Kirillov 63tl; Virunja 63tc; funnyangel 65; Brandon Bourdages 66b; Joe Dunckley 66t; alicja neumiler 67; Enigma AB 69; Esenin Studio 71; Dmitry Naumov 72; sanpom 73; Danler 74; James Greenshields 77; bioraven 78; Rudy Umans 79; OMMB 81; Darryl Sleath 82; Albert Michael Cutri 83b; plantic 84; Garsya 85; Deyan Georgiev 86b; Janelle Lugge 86t; Steve Buckley 87; Losonsky 88; Alison Hancock 89; Helen Franchuk 90; Nattapol Sritongcom 91; Vadym Zaitsev 92; Swellphotography 93; Alex Alekseev 94trb; Brent Hofacker 94bll, 201; Emily Goodwin 94tll; Fottostrazds 94brl; m.syafiq 94tlb; Manu M Nair 94tlr; Myibean 94brb; p_ponomareva 94brr; Paul Pellegrino 94trl; PRILL 94blr; Quanthem 94trr; Viktor Lugovskoy 94blb; Alicia G. Monedero 95t; topseller 96; Paul Hardwick Images 97; Przemyslaw Wasilewski 98; Wunigard 99; Rtimages 101; Ant Cooper 102; Howard Marsh 103; Simun Ascic 104t; Chris Warham 105t; EdBockStock 105b; onot 108 & 143t; Arina P Habich 111b; DoubleBubble 111t; Maria Dryfhout 111t; Jamie Hall 112; Indy Edge 113b; BasPhoto 114t; De_Macgog 114b; Svetlana Foote 115t; Tom Gowanlock 116; pxl.store 117t & 125t; WilleeCole Photography 118b; Gavin Young 119; James Hudson Photography 120; D. Pimborough 121, 135tl; Pim 126tr; BalkansCat 127t; nikolay100 128c; Visharo 128r; Amy McNabb 129c; Erika J Mitchell 129b; Miraleks 129t; Vladimir Wrangel 130; Brandt Bolding 131t; coreder 131b; Janice Adlarm 132b; Pete Gallop 132t; Janneke Spronk 133t; stockphoto mania 133b; tviolet 133c; iVangelos 134 & 135; l i g h t p o e t 134c; travelfoto 134tr; Eric Isselee 135b; Kevin Eaves 135tr; Chrispo 136b; Dick Kenny 136c; Menno Schaefer 136t; david muscroft 138; DianaFinch 138Br & 228; berdsigns 140tr & 174t; GreyDingo 140t; Martin Pateman 140b; Cameron Watson 141b; ChiccoDodiFC 141t; critterbiz 142t; Ralf Gosch 142t; stocksolutions 143b; BLUR LIFE 1975 147; tamarabegucheva 148; monticello 152; Jatinder1990 154; NatalyaBond 155; Anna Hoychuk 156b; marilyn barbone 157t; Davor Ristic 159b; Paul Gerritsen 159t; Jens Ottoson 161; Annika Olsson 162b; Chisoku 163; Andrew Buckin 164; Anton Havelaar 165b, 172b; Pixel Memoirs 165t; Karen Kaspar 166b; Leonid Ikan 166t; Mahyuddin 167t; Waddell Images 167b; Alexandra Cosmoss 168t; Elliot Photography 168bt; SFA Design 169bt; Mark William Richardson 170; Poly Liss 171; janecat 174bt; kristof lauwers 175bt; Paul Wishart 175t; aaltair 176; Janis Smits 177; Decent 178t; The Len 178b; kamira777 179; Alisa24 181; Peter Braakmann 182; MoreVector 183; Charles Amundson 186; Rawpixel.com 189; Pavel Ilyukhin 190; Dan Howell 191tt; Mureu 191tr; ymgerman 191b; Alliance 194b; melazerg 194t & 197b, 251t; Kondor83 195; Sasa Komlen 197t; Christopher Elwell 198; Wiktory 199; Geshas 200; mamita 202; Dudakova Elena 203; Foodpictures 204; denio109 205t; Robyn Mackenzie 205b; jarabee123 206; HandmadePictures 207b; JHK2303 208b; Thomas Oswald 208t; Marsan 212; Jat306 215; Paul Looyen 218; Zanna Demcenko 219b; Wuttichai jantarak 220; Neil Burton 221; Stephan Morris 222; Clicks by JB 223t; Mike Flippo 224; ESB Basic 225b; Pnor Tkk 225t; g-stockstudio 226; Minerva Studio 230; Modfos 232; RossHelen 233; Djem 234; sonya etchison 235t; Stephen Farhall 235b; Roman Babakin 236; Jacob Lund 237; Jose Ignacio Soto 238; Carlos Amarillo 239; NEIL ROY JOHNSON 240; Bildagentur Zoonar GmbH 242; focal point 244; DJTaylor 246; Jurga Jot 248; Graeme Dawes 249t; Teresa Neal 250; Tatiana Vorona 251; izzet ugutmen 270.

CREATE & MAINTAIN YOUR OWN

Smallholding

LIZ WRIGHT

FOREWORD BY
ROSEMARY CHAMPION

A GUIDE TO SUSTAINABLE SELF-SUFFICIENCY

FLAME TREE
PUBLISHING

Contents

It's a dream to live in the country, collect still-warm eggs and eat vegetables fresh from the garden. But should you make it a reality? Follow our pointers to find out if you have what it takes to become a smallholder. Should you take the plunge and move out into the country, or would making the most of where you are work for you? Only you can decide if smallholding remains a dream or becomes a lifestyle.

Starting smallholding begins long before you move. It starts with as much research and preparation as you can do. What should you look for in a smallholding? How many acres do you need? How will you find your perfect smallholding, and will you recognize it when you see it? Then there's the importance of paying attention to budgeting right from the beginning and other planning issues. This chapter includes a guide on how to view a smallholding and evaluate its advantages and disadvantages.

Growing on Your Land 60

This chapter focuses firstly on soil and pasture management – looking after that all-important grassland for your livestock, making hay and growing root crops for animal feed. There's even advice on buying a tractor. It then discusses growing home-grown crops to be either partly or fully self-sufficient, or just grow fruit and veg that are difficult or expensive to obtain in shops. We show you how to get your veg patch established, as well as looking at raised beds and other small-space growing, protected cropping to extend the seasons and organic growing.

Sourcing Livestock 108

First we look at what livestock and which breeds to keep, with brief descriptions of the main breeds of chickens, ducks, geese and turkeys. We cover all the popular smallholding breeds of pigs, sheep, goats and cattle, and take a look at alpacas. We've included tips on how to find the perfect livestock direct from breeders, through adverts or markets, and finally what to do when you get them home.

Keeping Livestock 150

This chapter highlights the five freedoms of livestock keeping and stockmanship, key to good welfare. We look at typical regulations on livestock keeping and the preparations you need to make before you buy. You'll learn how to keep your stock healthy, and the importance of avoiding overstocking. Then there's getting the best from your livestock, paying attention to their housing, grazing and feeding, and preventing disease and parasites. We tell you how to enrich your animals' environment to prevent boredom and allow them to show natural behaviour.

Reaping Your Rewards.... 184

This chapter shows you how to make the most of what you produce, whether it be to keep or to sell. We look at marketing and the options for selling, including going online to open up new markets; also farmers' markets, local markets and tapping into your workplace and friends and family to reach buyers. If you want to learn how to preserve your produce until next season, this chapter dips into jams, jellies, pickles, chutneys, fruit cheeses and sauces. Plus we take a look at preserving herbs, the traditional method of salting vegetables and storing and preserving eggs.

Pests and Problems

Don't panic, things can and do go wrong. In smallholding, there are some factors you just cannot control, but what do you do if you have a disaster, if your hens stop laying, the council are questioning your planning permissions, and rodents are overrunning your buildings? There is a solution to every problem if you know where to look. Prevention is always better than cure.

Taking Things Further

Smallholding can also take a more commercial turn, where more land is needed. Should you, can you, buy or rent? Plus we present the options for developing a new business by evaluating what you have on offer. You may be considering expanding into horses and donkeys on your holding, but are unsure of the implications – we point out key things to consider. We also look at a more natural way of cleaning, and foraging for seasonal food.

The Smallholding Year

Further Reading and Websites

Index

Foreword

For many people, to live on and work a smallholding is a lifetime's dream. It is both privilege and responsibility to steward the land for future generations. It's always advisable, then, to do some research before starting out.

Smallholders have a variety of objectives: some may want to simply spend a little time each day and a few hours at weekends producing some food for the family; others may want to make a living from land-based enterprises; or the goal may be something in between and change over time.

When we started our first smallholding in 2000, our aim was to produce food for ourselves. However, over the intervening 17 (how can it be 17?!) years, our enterprises have changed – from veggies and a few hens when we both worked full-time, to keeping hens, meat chickens, pigs, breeding sheep, and breeding and milking cattle. But it's been evolution, not revolution!

We still get a huge sense of satisfaction from eating a meal where most of the ingredients have been produced on our smallholding. It's also a huge buzz to be producing food for local people – we sell eggs, lamb and beef locally, knowing that we've cared for the animals and given them a good life, and our customers appreciate that. We also host visits from local primary schools, and watching children connect with food and where food comes from is very rewarding. And, of course, the highlights of the year are lambing and calving – the birth of new life. Smallholding is an amazing life, for sure.

Of course, there are downsides. The rewards of livestock keeping can be marred by accident, disease and death. Likewise, weather, disease and pests can damage your veggie crop irreparably. But it would be a bad year indeed if there were no successes in the garden. We've had years when our entire beetroot crop has been three beets and others where we've been pickling beetroot at midnight! Just go with the flow – reflect, learn and move on!

If I can give you, the aspiring smallholder, one piece of advice, it would be to record your progress – take photographs and keep a diary. It's easy to see only what still needs to be done and forget what you have achieved. Setting aside some time for reflection – in your veggie garden, your orchard or with your animals – is good for the soul, and smallholding is all about soul. Enjoy it.

Rosemary Champion
The Accidental Smallholder
www.accidentalsmallholder.net

Introduction

A 'smallholding' is a productive area of land that is smaller than a farm. The term has been known historically for many years. It's hard to be exactly sure when it started, whether the small blocks of land farmed by medieval peasants were the beginning of using small areas to feed your household, or whether the early nineteenth-century allotment movement was the true beginning.

Changes in the Social Landscape

In the UK in 1819, an Act of Parliament authorized the purchase of blocks of land of up to 22 acres to let to the poor and unemployed. In 1892, there was a Smallholdings Act in the UK. It allowed county councils to buy land for smallholdings and to this day, there are still county council smallholdings (though a diminishing number). In 1902, a national Small Holdings Association was formed, and in 1906, Land for the People Ltd was set up by the Salvation Army. 'Three acres and a cow' has long been a precious dream and, for some, a reality. A total of 14,045 smallholders were settled on the land between 1908 and 1914. Meanwhile, in North America, huge land settlement had been going on for hundreds of years, with the settlers having to learn new skills to be self-sufficient in a new country. A 'homesteader' is the rough American equivalent of a 'smallholder'.

The World Wars

And then the First World War came, which had a huge effect on smallholdings in the UK. The tenants were often away fighting, an unconscionable number of whom never returned, and many of the holdings became neglected. But after the war, there was a great move to relocate ex-servicemen on the land. The Land Settlement (Facilities) Act (1919) had a fund of £20 million to buy and equip smallholdings to be divided into fruit farms, market gardens and dairy farms. Around 2,400 ex-servicemen were settled, but that still didn't meet the demand.

It was perhaps at this time that the interest in smallholding was at its highest. It was not plain sailing, with various degrees of success in how well the smallholdings were run, and considerable intervention from the interested parties, but it is at this time that there was the most literature on smallholding. *The Smallholder* magazine, which turned into a gardening magazine before ceasing publication in the 1960s, was launched in 1910 and had thousands of subscribers. There were numerous books published as well. Then the Second World War further fuelled the desire to produce food at home.

Renewed Enthusiasm

However, after the war, the smallholding movement fell out of favour, especially in the 1960s with the development of the more industrial type of farming. It was left to a group of new enthusiasts in the 1970s to pick up the baton. John Seymour inspired a new generation with his book about self-sufficiency. Poultry keeping and, above all, goat keeping were rediscovered and more smallholding magazines were launched. There was a remarkable resemblance to their predecessors, with the emphasis on small-scale farming, but less attention paid to making a profit. It was more about self-sufficiency, growing without chemicals and in line with nature.

The Modern Model

Today's smallholders work the land in much the same way as those who have gone before: working with the seasons, taking pride in production and a having a particular interest in poultry. But in most cases, we are not smallholding to provide our main form of income, but to give us a quality of life that cannot be found elsewhere; smallholding to take some control over how we source our food and to know the provenance of what we eat.

Today, there are so many models of smallholding, from the more traditional small farm to the market garden (which is perhaps the most reliable method of making an income), or even a part-time smallholding that fits around our lifestyle but still provides us with food and a sense of wellbeing.

Choose Your Own Model

In this book, we look at all aspects of modern smallholding and how to make modern technology, such as the internet, work to your advantage. We explore the many different things you can do on your land and how you can take them further.

Many methods have improved, so we no longer have to worry about fowl pest destroying our chicken flock, and modern wormers and vaccines can help to keep our flock in tip-top condition. There is also an organic movement, which does not preclude the use of modern medicine if necessary, but aims to work with nature to produce the highest standards of animal management and health. For most smallholders, the path lies somewhere in between.

Doing It Differently

Smallholders do not push their livestock and crops to over-produce, they often grow heritage varieties of vegetables and fruit trees, and look for rare-breed livestock that has the characteristics of hardiness and ease of reproduction. This way, they are the guardians of the past, the keepers of the national gene bank, so that if commercial farming changes (and it has), those genes will still be there to use.

Smallholders keep the old methods going, blending the old and the new, learning traditional skills but sometimes running them alongside modern methods.

Smallholders care about their land and want to encourage wildlife to share their fields. They produce a number of crops that help to feed the pollinators such as the bees, and keep traditional small paddocks with hedges that feed so much wildlife.

Doing It With Pride

You want to be a smallholder? Be proud to be one, as farming's heritage and future is as much your responsibility as it is any farmer's. Learn all you can before you start and always put the welfare of your livestock before anything else. Enjoy your lifestyle and share with others. In knowing where your food originates and being able to produce it yourself, you are in a special position indeed, but always remember:

Take only what you need and you will thrive
Take too much and you won't survive!

Advice to Would-Be Smallholders

▶ **Explore all the options:** There are no two smallholdings alike. Choose what will work best for you and your family.

▶ **Enter with enthusiasm:** This will take you far, but remember you will also need a sound financial plan.

▶ **Do your homework:** Learn as much as you can before you begin, and certainly before you start buying up land and filling it with animals.

▶ **Start your smallholding before you move:** What's a windowsill for but to grow things on? Raised beds can fit into a very small garden.

▶ **Join a smallholding club:** If there isn't one in your area, think about starting one. Visit livestock shows, smallholdings, farm open days; if you're in the town, tap into the city farm movement to learn and get experiences. Offer to be a steward at a show for the inside experience.

▶ **Never overstock or take on too much:** This won't be good for your own or your animals' welfare.

▶ **Enjoy your new life to the full!** Perhaps the most important advice of all. Smallholding presents many challenges, but every one tackled brings reward and experience.

Is Smallholding for You?

Think Before You Leap

Although there are things you can do where you currently live, town or country, moving to a place with some land is a big step towards becoming a smallholder. But before you up sticks and move, take time to consider the implications and to think about what your expectations are, and what you want from the experience.

The Dream

If your dream is to have a slower pace of life, work fewer hours and make money, then smallholding probably isn't for you. If you imagine yourself lying back on the warm grass, dozing as the bees buzz around you, this can and does happen, but it is a rare moment indeed for the average smallholder.

The Reality

However, if you see yourself taking control of part of your life with regards to food production and energy use, working with nature (and sometimes against!) in the quest to grow food, and integrating into a new community, then you have a more realistic vision.

Reasons for Becoming Self-Sufficient

▶ **Traceability:** It's a wonderful thing to know exactly where your food comes from.

▶ **Food security:** This phrase was once only heard in developing countries, but it is now of concern to each and every one of us.

▶ **Save on the household food budget:** Especially by growing the more unusual vegetables and salad leaves that are expensive in the supermarket.

▶ **To reduce food miles:** You can't get much less than from garden to kitchen!

▶ **To reduce our carbon footprint:** Lessen our impact on the earth by By producing locally, ecologically and effectively.

▶ **Ensuring animal welfare:** You'll learn the best and most humane methods of animal husbandry.

▶ **To get the freshest taste:** Much has been argued about whether home-produced food really tastes better, but everyone who grows their own agrees it certainly does!

▶ **To educate:** Younger family members will have the opportunity to learn where food really comes from.

▶ **To get fit:** This is healthy outdoor exercise that produces more than just a sweat!

▶ **To reconnect:** Re-establish a bond with the land and with our past.

▶ **To gain a new appreciation:** By doing it yourself, you'll realize all the effort, skill and knowledge that goes into producing food.

▶ **To meet like-minded people:** Swap ideas and experiences and make friends.

What Is a Smallholding?

Traditionally, a smallholding has been thought of as a few acres, usually under 10 but often as little as one acre, that has a small number of crops and livestock. The main intention is to be self-sufficient in food and if possible fuel as well, and have a surplus to take to market.

Born of Necessity

In the glory days of smallholding between the wars and just after the Second World War, these holdings usually had the base of a market garden, where cash crops were grown for sale. Animals that could thrive on a smaller acreage were also kept. The staple was poultry of all kinds with laying hens as an almost year-round source of money, Christmas poultry and table birds, and rabbits for meat. Goats would supply milk and meat. Pigs would be fed on excess milk from the goats and the market garden and were also kept for meat. A small orchard would normally also be part of the smallholding.

Still Relevant Today

Even today, this model would work quite well as a full-time smallholding with good marketing and proximity to a town to sell the surplus. The rise of farmers' markets and the growth in village shops and community enterprises are once again opening up outlets for direct sale from smallholder to consumer.

More Than Food

But smallholding is more of a way of life than a defined amount of land and livestock. It has changed over history, becoming tailored to the needs and expectations of the people living on it. These days, smallholding is usually associated with free-range livestock and organic or sustainable growing with minimal use of chemicals. Although normally thought of as 'mixed' farming with both livestock and crops, due to pressures of work which make caring for livestock impossible, many people nowadays are concentrating on orchards and polytunnels, which, although they need work, do not need round-the-clock care. Smallholding is a means of achieving self-sufficiency – in reality, this is more likely to be partial self-sufficiency for most people – and this can be achieved both in town and in the country. The programme 'The Good Life' from the 1970s showed just such a town garden that was run as a smallholding, but highlighted a lot of the challenges too.

What Is Self-Sufficiency?

Today, the words 'food security' are increasingly being used. In Britain, for example, 30 years ago, the country produced 80 per cent of its own food, but now it is 60 per cent – a dangerous trend. It is said that, at present, approximately 16 per cent of people totally rely on food produced outside their country and this figure will increase. In an uncertain world, it is encouraging to think that you can rely on your own land to produce at least some of your food requirements.

Why Is It Important?

But it is not just about the practicalities of producing some of your own food. Anyone who grows or rears their own can never look at food in the same way, knowing the effort required and the challenges with nature and the seasons. For a child, this is particularly valuable. Not only can they recognize where food on their plate originates, they also have a respect for it. A chicken is not just a lump of tasteless white meat, coated in synthetic spices, but a living being. Picking a sweetcorn and then eating it grilled is a real thrill. Not only have you given your children life skills, you have given them a respect for life.

Urban Smallholdings

Don't wait for the idyllic rural plot. Start now, with a windowsill if you have no garden. A small garden can produce a surprising amount of food if carefully planned, and the help of a small greenhouse can really push the boundaries. If you're lucky, most villages and towns have allotments or community gardens, where you can grow food and also develop a real camaraderie with fellow growers (though you may have to be on a long waiting list).

From Small Beginnings

In 1910, the first year of *The Smallholder* magazine, a reader wrote in from the town saying that he had two hens and a small veg plot and asking was he now a smallholder? The editor replied that he was "well on his way". That's over a hundred years ago and we are now returning to the idea that we can produce some of our food even in small areas and we don't all need to be living in the countryside.

Twenty-First-Century Smallholding

It is almost a contradiction that, amidst the hustle and bustle of modern life, many people are craving a slower, quieter way of life where they can produce food, fuel and even crafts. In many ways, this aspiration goes against the trend of consumerism and the throwaway society.

Prepare for New Challenges

However, it is not likely to be quite as quiet or stress-free as the escapee to the country might think! There is nothing calming about being totally out of control with the weather, caring for sick animals, staying up night after night lambing or even nervously looking at your bank account. But there are compensations in the form of working outside and listening to the sounds of the countryside, working with the seasons and weather and forging strong links to work with others or market your products. A good dose of realism is needed to get the foundations of your new life established. Spending

'The facts as they stand are sufficiently indicative of the greater productive possibilities of small than large holdings.' *The Practical Smallholder*, Volume I (*c.* 1930)

more time on your own (and maybe with your family) means you get to know yourself (and them) much better. You can learn what your skills are and learn new ones, using them to their best advantage.

Modern Technology

You may be hankering for a simpler life, but don't throw out the modern technology. It really does make smallholding much easier in so many ways. You can look up the ideas you have and thoroughly research them, plus talk directly to people online to learn from their experiences. Want to grow plants for cut flowers for example? You can check out who is doing it and what they are growing, check out the costs of the flowers and even learn about the management of soil types.

Smallholders Online

Social media helps you to keep in touch with smallholders everywhere – nearly all smallholding clubs have both a Facebook page and a website. It makes it easier to source products and materials for your smallholding – from jam jars for preserves and honey to sheep hurdles. It even helps you look for stock, but do remember, it is still best to go and look for yourself. The selling sites on the internet offer outlets for your crafts or your business, and you can set up online shops. If you don't have internet skills, find a short course locally and learn, as they are so useful in the smallholding world.

Should I Stay or Should I Go?

In the twenty-first century, it is much easier to grow and keep livestock in the town or even city than it was in the latter part of the twentieth century. Chicken keeping has become fashionable and, if neighbours are happy and the chickens are well kept, even a small garden can accommodate a few bantams.

The square-metre method.

City Facilities

New techniques of growing have revolutionized how small spaces can be used. Two examples are the square-metre/foot method, where you divide a small plot up into squares and sow successionally; and vertical gardening, where you grow up as well as down. Another new development gaining popularity is landshare, where someone with some spare land rents, loans or even co-manages the area with others. There is the transition network to help to bring small growers and farmers together. The city farm movement has larger farm animals, often in the heart of inner cities. So there are options to stay where you are but increase your smallholding skills.

Weighing Up What You've Got

Ask the following questions to help you decide whether to stay put or move to fresh fields:

▶ How much land is actually available to me?

▶ Can I fit in a small greenhouse or grow things in a different way, such as vertically or in containers?

▶ Am I using all the land that I actually have or can I alter it to create more space?

▶ What is acceptable in the area I live; for example, can I keep poultry such as bantams or quail?

Vertical gardening.

▶ What type of soil is the land – heavy, medium, light, sandy?

▶ Can the land be worked all year round or does it get too wet or too dry?

▶ Is the land sheltered or exposed?

▶ How much time is there every day for routine care of crops or livestock?

▶ Are there some parts of the year when I can find more or less time?

▶ Are all my family keen to help or is most of the work going to come down to me?

27

Know Yourself

There are as many ways to run a smallholding as there are smallholdings, and what you keep, what you grow and what you make will depend on your skill set, your personal likes and dislikes, and your dreams – probably in that order.

Decide What Is Important to You

Be brutally honest. It might be a comparatively small ambition such as collecting a fresh, warm egg every day. Or you might want to take the plunge and be almost totally self-supporting, if not immediately then in the future. Both are quite possible, but it is always best to plan, start small and grow.

What Skills Do You Have?

Again, be honest. If you are a competent mechanic, then your self-sufficiency may involve more machinery in its approach. Perhaps you are a talented cook – which may lead to producing jams and chutneys and selling at farmers' markets. So often, we overlook the things we are really good at because we take them for granted. Get your partner or friends to list your skills; you will be surprised at what you have. What skills do you have in your job? Are you good at IT, networking or promotion? All are useful skills if you decide to run a small

business. Never underestimate the ability to just get on with people; this in itself is a useful skill for marketing.

What's Your Natural Personality?

Are you outgoing? If you are, bartering, trading and perhaps having people to your smallholding will work well for you. Or does the thought of never having to see anyone again fill you with joy? In that case, marketing might have to be done strictly via the internet while you talk to your sheep!

Are You Squeamish?

If so, don't have breeding animals! If you are not sure, go on a hands-on course to see how you cope with birth, life and death.

How Do You Really Feel About Killing For Food?

If you really hate the idea, why not just major on vegetables and crafts? You shouldn't force yourself to do something that goes against your nature. There is no rule that says all self-sufficiency must be exactly the same; you need to make it work for you. Hens don't need a cockerel and hybrid hens don't raise chicks, so no possibility of unwanted cockerels. There are vegan and vegetarian smallholders who adapt what they grow and produce to their lifestyle.

Work With Your Health

Although there are health benefits to being outside and taking more exercise – to say nothing of eating all the lovely fresh food you produce – self-sufficiency is hard work, so just be careful about what you take on.

Know Your Limits

If you have any health issues, choose less demanding projects. You can adapt your smallholding to make it easier to work. Raised beds are much easier for anyone with arthritis or back pain. When it comes to livestock, for example, all sheep require some physical effort, but they do come in different

"'My other piece of advice, Copperfield,' said Mr. Micawber, 'you know. Annual income twenty pounds, annual expenditure nineteen pounds six, result happiness. Annual income twenty pounds, annual expenditure twenty pounds ought and six, result misery.'"

David Copperfield,
Charles Dickens (1850)

sizes. If you suffer with any physical problems, it might help to choose smaller, more docile breeds, just in consideration of weight when turning over to trim feet or crutching out. Or consider buying a sheep cradle that will help you to turn them.

Be Realistic About Money

Budget carefully and ideally get someone who is already smallholding to check your figures. Try to keep some form of regular income as you set up your smallholding. Expenses of feeding and caring for livestock are very high, and there are vet expenses to account for too.

Checklist

Consider all the factors: Be sure about what you want to achieve.

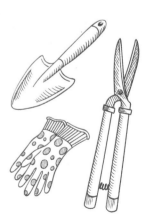

▶ **Be honest with your skills:** Remember to include transferable skills such as accounting, marketing and computer skills.

▶ **Make sure everyone is on board:** Are all the family keen to make the move?

▶ **Budget carefully:** Will it work financially?

▶ **Location:** Can you achieve what you want by not moving?

Getting Ready

Planning to Succeed

Planning starts before you move: choosing your smallholding, learning the right skills, understanding all the legal requirements, thinking about what equipment you need, and what all this is likely to cost.

Finding Your Smallholding

Most people have an idea which area of the country they want to settle. A few are guided by what is available and the cost of smallholdings. Fewer and fewer areas offer land and houses at low prices, but if you decide to move for price of land alone, then do visit several times before committing yourself to live somewhere not known to you.

There are still a few areas in the UK which are cheaper, though there are usually reasons for this, such as a lack of jobs in the area or the inability to commute easily to a larger town or city. These areas may well suit you if you don't need to earn a good salary, and they often have strong local communities.

Looking Further Afield

For the more adventurous, land and houses in parts of Europe are often much cheaper, but don't underestimate the language barrier and be prepared to learn it as soon as you can. Always take into consideration the local customs of anywhere you move. Don't move into an area where you find any of the practices disturbing or where the neighbours are not to your liking. If you move next to a large industrial unit, they are not going to stop operating because you find their noise overpowering in the early mornings.

Sources For Smallholdings

Online, of course! There are dedicated smallholding/rural estate agents that will come up on a search. More mainstream online sources do have properties with land; if you put the right filters in for land then you won't have to look through hundreds of town properties.

▶ Private sellers: Again, an online search will often show these properties.

▶ Local papers: Although their influence is fading, some local papers still have good property sections and also give a feel of the area you are considering.

▶ Taking a look yourself: Visit estate agents in the towns near to where you want to locate and have a drive round the area. At the very least, you'll learn more about it and you may spot a property!

▶ Contact the local smallholding club: It's worth checking to see if there's a smallholding club in the area where you want to move. The secretary will point you in the right direction.

Smallholding Technicalities

Although there is no legal definition of a smallholding, it is generally taken to mean an area of land of between one and 10 acres that is worked by the owner and their family. In the UK, sometimes properties are described as a 'registered smallholding', which means that they have an agricultural holding number (CPH). You would need to have this number whether you had a thousand acres or one acre, so it doesn't usually affect planning matters.

What Is a CPH number?

CPH stands for County Parish Holding. The number is an identification number for your farm or business, which relates to the location of the land. It's a nine-digit number (for example, 12/345/6789). The first two digits relate to the county, the next three relate to the parish and the last four digits identify the holding.

Its main purpose is to identify and trace the location of livestock. Contact the RPA (Rural Payments Agency), who will guide you through how to apply or look up an existing number.

Keeping Farmed Animals

If you keep one or more of the following, you will need a number:

- ▶ Cattle (including bison and buffalo)
- ▶ Deer
- ▶ Sheep
- ▶ Goats
- ▶ Pigs
- ▶ Poultry (more than 50 birds)

Working Out Your Priorities

You can help your search by focusing in on a few key factors. Where you want to live is naturally high up on the list, but as this is a move to live on the land, what you can grow on what amount of land of what type are all crucial considerations.

Quality Versus Quantity

The type of land directly influences what you can produce: five acres of thin soil on the side of a mountain is not going to grow as much as, say, half an acre in a lowland area of rich, well-drained soil. Therefore it is impossible to say exactly what you can do on an acre, for example, without knowing the soil type, drainage, position and layout.

▶ **Drainage:** This is especially important. If the area is under water for half the year, that will severely restrict land use.

37

▶ **Position:** Think of the difference between a sheltered holding in a sunny area compared with a holding on an island by the sea where wind is a real issue.

▶ **Incline:** Level land is easier to work than steep land, which will be hard to reach with machinery and will limit what you can do on the land.

Top Tip

The best plan when you first keep livestock is to start small and grow. Don't overstock.

Many smallholdings will have a mixture – some level, well-drained paddocks and some rougher, wetter grazing – but the type of land and soil will make a difference to what you can do on it and how much you can produce.

Location, Location, Location

This is as much of a factor as it is in the residential property market. The less useful and further from a town the land is, the cheaper it is likely to be. A market-garden type smallholding based around fresh fruit and vegetables, cut flowers, poultry and eggs and perhaps bees, needs to be near a market in order to sell produce.

One Acre Versus Five Acres or More

Despite the caveats above, generally the more land you have, the more you can do and produce. Here follows a comparison of what you can do with a smaller versus a larger smallholding.

The One-Acre Smallholding

On a smallholding of around one to a few acres, depending on the quality of the grass, the drainage and the situation, you could consider some of the following options:

▶ Polytunnel: This is top of the list for a reason! It's an essential on any successful smallholding. Your polytunnel will give you the ability to produce a wide range of crops for your family plus surplus to sell, as well as support specialist enterprises such as bedding plants, hanging baskets and cut flowers. Carefully planned (and maintained), the polytunnel will provide income as well as produce. Just be careful because a polytunnel requires planning permission in many areas, so check first. However, this hurdle seems mainly to be to deter the big commercial growers in picturesque areas.

▶ **Greenhouse:** This will allow a variety of crops to be sown earlier in the year, giving them a good start, plus it will allow you to grow on fruit and vegetables (i.e. give seedlings a chance to develop).

▶ **A small orchard:** Grow trees of top fruits (top fruit is that which grows on trees, as opposed to soft fruit) and a soft fruit bed for use in the house. Sell or preserve any surplus.

▶ **A large vegetable garden:** Ideal if it's of a scale that can grow marketable crops such as asparagus (a good cash crop for the spring) and strawberries (bringing in summer income).

▶ **A herb bed:** For use in the kitchen with the possibility of drying surplus.

▶ **Compost:** This can be made on a wider scale from more materials.

▶ **Water:** Collection of rainwater and use of grey water can be expanded.

▶ **Scaled-up poultry:** Numbers can be increased from garden poultry and ducks can be considered, as can geese (who will be a real help in the orchard eating fallen fruits).

40

▶ **Turkeys:** These birds not only produce meat for the festive season, but there is also a market for their large and delicious eggs. Quality rare breeds can achieve a good price as breeding stock.

▶ **An apiary:** If you can establish a bee colony, this will help pollinate the orchard and plants.

▶ **Weaners:** Piglets that are ready to leave their mothers and no longer suckle can be raised to bacon or pork weight for the freezer (see the section on pigs in Sourcing Livestock).

▶ **Goats:** It may be possible to keep a pair for dairying and for meat.

▶ **Lambs:** Consider the possibility of rearing a few orphans for the freezer, but they will need a grass field for finishing after you have weaned them. If you are rearing for meat, it is far more effective to buy in the young animal and rear it than go in for breeding livestock.

41

▶ **Sustainable and renewable energy:** In the house, think about a log burner and consider alternative energy ideas such as a wind turbine.

More Than a Few Acres

This gives you more flexibility, but still it's best start with small numbers. Among the many things you could do on a larger amount of land (say, five to 20 acres), you could:

▶ **Keep breeding livestock:** This requires a much higher level of livestock management skill and a knowledge of livestock breeds. Where the smallholder can capitalize is by developing real knowledge of specific breeds and breeding the best animals they can, so that there is a market for quality breeding animals as well as the meat market. This obviously takes time to learn and to develop, but it's worth having this thought in mind when you select your breeds initially. Think too about breeding rare breeds and take time to research their unique points. There's also a market for rare-breed meat if properly presented, as well as the benefit to your own freezer. Rare-breed pigs offer great potential, as most of these breeds were originally the choice of smallholders and have fallen out of favour in commercial systems.

▶ **Keep cattle:** They do require good grass and you do not want to have too many, but a house cow (*see* page 179) or a couple of calves for fattening would be a possibility.

▶ **Goats:** As well as for dairy, you could keep a larger number for meat and for fibre (e.g. Angora or Cashmere) – as long as your fencing is very good. Remember goats like to browse rather than just graze.

▶ **Keep camelids:** These delightful animals (such as alpacas) produce quality fibre and llamas can also be used as pack animals, perhaps for a small trekking business.

▶ **Grow fodder:** This will provide your animals with food for the winter in the form of hay, haylage or silage. Hay requires good weather but is the safest method of conservation. This depends on having enough land available per animal for both grazing and fodder conservation and on keeping livestock off the hay field throughout the non-growing period.

▶ **Grow alternative fodder:** For example, mangolds/mangelwurzels, fodder turnips and beet (*see* page 74). These will not replace a concentrate ration but will bulk out the diet.

▶ **Grow vegetables on a greater scale:** For example, onions or potatoes for sale by the net or sack.

▶ **Grow cereals:** For bread making.

▶ **Keep a horse:** For help on the smallholding. A horse could be trained to pull a cart, go logging or pull a plough. This requires considerable skill, but for those of an equestrian leaning may be a very useful option for semi-retired children's ponies or a ride/drive cob.

43

Other Considerations

You can see there's a lot to think about even before you start looking at smallholdings, and there are other factors that can be easily overlooked but which may prove crucial once you've committed to a plot of land. Some considerations may not be obvious at the planning stage, others may be have been avoided because they're unpalatable to think about.

How Much Food Will Your Family Need?

It's a humbling but interesting exercise to work out exactly how much a family will eat in a year and then see what proportion you will be able to produce by integrating your smallholding with livestock and vegetables. How many chickens does your family eat a year? How many eggs? What percentage of fruit? What could they eat more of? What could they eat less of? In order to plan your holding, you need to have some idea of your market requirements – in this case, your family.

Will They Eat What You Produce?

What are your family's needs and wants? Will they drink goat's milk? If not, then you might be better off with a cow, depending on the fodder available. Will your family eat home-raised poultry?

Can You Afford to be Sentimental?

What livestock are you 'carrying'? Yes, your much-loved riding horse is a 'burden' to the smallholding, eating large amounts of grass and hay, taking your time and only providing some manure in return. Be realistic as to how much of your land this will take. If you only have an acre, the horse will need all of this and more unless you buy in hay and restrict the grazing (often not practical or welfare friendly). The larger the horse, the more it will 'poach' (damage) the grass in wet weather, and as horses should have a companion, it's likely these problems will be doubled. There's nothing wrong in being fond of your livestock and keeping neutered male goats and sheep, but they are unproductive in terms of income. In reality, many smallholdings have animals that have other uses such as companionship or riding as well as the productive livestock, but you need to make sure that if you are trying to earn some income, you allow in your budget for animals that won't earn anything.

Have You Got Mechanical Know-How?

What machinery will you need? How much do you know about tractors? Most tractors are woefully underused and are capable of doing a great many more tasks than their owners realize. What do you want to do with the tractor? Tow a trailer, use a front loader, make hay, chop wood? You decide and then look for a tractor that is versatile.

45

Making a List

You've thought about what skills you have and your family's needs, but now it's time to think about what you really want and make your wish list. There probably isn't a smallholding in the world that fulfils every wish, but listing your must-haves and nice-to-haves does help you focus on what you want and not get carried away by a lovely view or a chocolate-box house.

A Case Study

Mel and Simon have three children aged two, five and seven. He is a freelance designer and she was previously an art teacher but would like to specialize in stained glass. They want to raise their own pigs and poultry and develop an orchard. They feel they cannot be too far from London, as their parents are getting older. Their wish list may look like this:

Essential

▶ **Fast broadband** so Simon is able to continue his work.

▶ **A spare room or outbuilding** for Mel to develop her stained-glass business.

▶ **Within two hours or less of London** with easy commuting.

▶ **Well-drained land of at least an acre** to be able to rotate free-range pigs from weaners to freezer and allow for possible future breeding of rare breed pigs.

▶ **Suitable land for planting an orchard.**

▶ **Good schools nearby,** including a preschool.

▶ **Off the main road** with safe play area.

▶ **Within reach of the village community** so children can have friends locally.

Desirable

▶ **As much land** as can be afforded.

▶ **Greenhouse or polytunnel.**

▶ **Garden area** already developed.

▶ **Good-size kitchen.**

'Would Be Nice'

▶ **Good views** over the countryside.

▶ **Hedging** and woodland.

▶ **Wood burners** in the house.

▶ **Two bathrooms.**

> 'Although it is by no means always possible to select the most suitable situation for a smallholding, it is necessary to have a sufficient knowledge of the factors that make for success.'
> *The Practical Smallholder*
> (*c.* 1930)

The 'would be nice' list is likely to be something that you could do to a property after moving, while the essentials – such as being two hours from London – is something you cannot change after moving.

Financial Planning

Thinking about what you really need and want is the obvious first step. The next, how you are going to pay for it, is of course crucial to achieving those desires. Money is probably the biggest potential pitfall, but there's one other that can cause many a smallholder to come unstuck.

Stick To Your Budget

Money, or rather lack of it, is the number one reason would-be smallholders do not succeed and, worse still, become disaffected. The budget is the single most important thing to get right and the one that so many people miscalculate. It isn't the maths that's at fault, it's just what happens when enthusiasm quite naturally overtakes reality. Be absolutely sure that you have done your sums right for moving – the

move itself, the stamp duty, the solicitors' fees, the estate agent's fees and other incidentals – and what you need for the future. If anything, overestimate the costs of moving and setting up. Above all, do not estimate your income from anything but your job and especially not from your new smallholding. Whatever plot you decide to buy will have to be paid for out of the money you have available – don't overreach yourself.

Seek Out the Hidden Costs

The hidden costs of smallholding include insurance. It's more expensive to insure outside buildings than a straightforward three-bedroom house in a village. Check out the costs. You'll also need to cover tractors and machinery, and livestock will need at least third-party insurance, so if they cause an accident you are not liable financially. If you have anyone coming to your smallholding, you will have to consider public liability. If you are employing anyone, then that brings a new set of insurances.

> 'Money is not the only answer, but it makes a difference.'
> **Barack Obama**

Watch out also for the cost of bases for buildings – concreting is quite expensive – and also for preserving new-build wood with wood preservative. If you have to spray any land for weeds, unless you have the necessary certificates, you'll have to pay someone and herbicides are themselves costly. Check out machinery and equipment costs before finalizing the budget. No longer do second-hand tractors sit waiting for a buyer to take them off their owners' hands; they have become very competitively priced due to the thriving vintage market. Do your maths homework thoroughly.

Failing to Plan Is Planning to Fail

Planning permission is the second contender in the 'I wish I had known that before I started' category, just after 'I wish I had fully calculated the costs'. Lives have been ruined by not paying attention to planning considerations. Never assume you will get planning permission unless you have it there in writing. 'Believed to be able to get planning' means just that – it's a belief, not a fact. If something has outline planning, then carefully check it and make sure it hasn't expired.

Changing Uses

Planning is not just about buildings, but also relates to change of activities and land use (to and from agricultural, for example). It also can include polytunnels and greenhouses for commercial use, camping and caravanning and even running bed and breakfasts. In some areas, especially national parks, there are additional rules, so check them out first.

Generally domestic uses of land such as keeping a few chickens or even a couple of weaners won't raise too many eyebrows, but as soon as they become a bigger business, they may well need different forms of planning. Be absolutely sure that what you want to do will be within the planning guidelines. Even providing your household with alternative energy such as domestic windmills or solar panels usually carries a planning implication.

Seek Local Knowledge

Always take advice first, before even moving let alone before laying the first brick. Even within countries or areas, some districts are more amenable than others to smallholders, so there are no hard-and-fast rules. A conversation with the local smallholders' club is likely to tell you what kind of planning authority

you are moving into. You can also call in and see the local planners at the council before you buy.

Know Your Rights of Way

You must abide by existing planning law and rights of way. If your property has a right of way across it, you must maintain it and allow access. It's up to you to decide whether you view this as an intrusion or an advantage, and either buy or not buy. What you can't do is try to close rights of way when you have moved. See the next section for more on rights of way.

Viewing the Smallholding

Fully prepared, knowing what you want from the property and land, and with a budget in your head, now is the time to start viewing. First impressions do count. If you really hate the area and take an instant dislike, it probably won't improve whatever you try to tell yourself.

Question Everything

Photos can distort the truth and sometimes estate agents leave out vital facts, such as a railway line running at the bottom of the land, or that 'easy access to nearest town' means it's on a main road that is busy all day and night. Question estate agents before making long journeys. Ask whether there is anything else they can tell you, for example, proximity to main road, industrial area, rail or anything else you particularly dislike living next to. Take something to make notes on and a camera to record things you can look at again later.

51

Keep an Open Mind

Ignore all those property programmes that talk about presentation and remember this is someone's home, so look beyond the decoration, the ornaments and the general clutter of everyday life. Picture the property empty and ready for you to put your stamp on it.

Look at the Land First

For a smallholding, the land itself is going to be the most important factor in what you can do. First of all, is it flat, gently sloping or is it so steep you'll need a chair lift to get to the top? Steep ground does look lovely, but do you want to climb up it every day, maybe twice a day, to check your stock? The gradient also limits what machinery (if any) you can use, due to the danger of tractors tipping over.

Drainage

Where does the water drain? Follow the plot down to the bottom and check to see if the land has been waterlogged. Telltale signs of excessive water are marshy type grasses and plants, cracking, and hoof marks left from last season's grazing. If the land is very wet in the winter, then there will be months of the year when it is out of action, although it might produce a good hay crop if the summer is not too wet.

Top Tip

Try to imagine how the smallholding would look and feel in rain and wind.

Barns Are Your Best Friend

You can never have too many buildings! You will certainly need to have some buildings, even if you are not going to keep livestock. When looking at smallholdings, take a good look at the barns, stables and livestock areas.

The Beauty of Outbuildings

Buying a smallholding with a good range of buildings will:

▶ **Save you money**, as you won't need to build.

▶ Save you the challenges of getting **planning permission**, or the risk of having it refused.

53

▶ Mean you can **get started straight away**.

▶ **Might bring you in extra money** in the future, for example, if you obtained planning permission for residential use.

Inside Outbuildings

Check the outdoor buildings against the property listing. Check the sizes and the condition of the buildings. Look inside. A 10-metre by 10-metre building may not be such a useful size if it has girders inside holding it up which reduce the available space. Also think about the height of the building – can you get machinery inside or stack hay? What constructions are the buildings? What sort of condition are they in? Do they need repairing? Take some photos and dimensions. The floor, too, is important: concrete is expensive, so any buildings that come with a well-laid concrete floor will be an asset.

Outside Outbuildings

Take a look at the outside as well. A well-built barn, although helpful, is much better if the yard outside is dry and is of a material that drains and can stand having machinery parked on it or animals walking on it. How far are the buildings from the house? Think about walking from the house to the buildings in the middle of winter. For lambing, for example, you will want to have the barn as close as possible, as you'll be doing night-time checks.

Be Secure

Time to pretend to be a burglar! Look at the buildings through the eyes of someone wanting to get in. Are they in view of the house? Can you get in from the back of the buildings without being seen? Are they secure in terms of being able to be shut and locked? How visible and close to the road are they? A yard that has good fencing with perhaps a ditch on all sides and only one entrance is going to be far more secure than somewhere which can be accessed by coming across the fields.

Good Fences Make Good Neighbours

The need to have secure boundaries in the form of fences and gates is also important. If not already erected, you will need to budget for this and good fencing is expensive. Even if you do it yourself, you'll still have to cover the cost of the materials, so look carefully at the total cost.

Let There Be Light!

Is there any form of outside lighting? Being able to light up outbuildings really helps for security – motion-activated lights are a good option. If you work during the day, then good lighting in the dark is not a luxury but a necessity for your return home, otherwise you are relying on head torches and battery power. You can achieve this with solar power these days, as lighting without access to the grid is constantly developing. But if you have electricity, this is a bonus and also gives you access to sockets, which you can use for incubators or deep freezes. It's worth getting electric wiring checked out by an electrician, as it doesn't last as well outside as inside the house. Check, too, that it is on a separate circuit so if you have a mouse eat through a cable, your whole house isn't plunged into darkness. Many systems have a circuit breaker built in, which means if something is dangerous to the system – such as if you cut through a wire – it switches off.

On Track For Success

The final outside check is for rights of way over the property. The legal rights of way can be seen on a map and will come up in a property search. If you don't like the idea of a right of way, then don't buy the property as you cannot change them and certainly cannot block them. You have to have a really good reason to divert them and many applications are unsuccessful. They can be a real advantage if you want to sell

Top Tip

Never ever buy a piece of land and assume you will get planning if you start a smallholding. If it were that easy, everyone would do it.

drinks or food and can be a positive asset if you run a horse yard. Check whether they are footpaths (people only), bridleways (people and ridden horses), or byways, which allow wheeled vehicles, either motorized or horse-drawn.

Be particularly vigilant for informal rights of way, such as a track used by the village for years but not on the map, or a cut-through. These are not always as easy to bring to an end as people think. Also look for any legal rights by neighbours over your land, and do check whether any sporting rights are sold with the property, otherwise you may be surprised when the shooting season starts.

The Heart of a Smallholding

You may think the house is not as important as the outside and in some ways you might be right. Many new smallholders start off in a caravan or mobile home, rebuilding an existing house. But just pause to consider if you will have the time, especially if you are working, to get the smallholding up and running and renovate a house. The costs of house-building always seem to be more than budgeted and you need to take account of what the final value of the property would be.

Working Areas

Pay careful attention to the kitchen and storage area. You may want to do a lot of storing and preserving, so a good-size kitchen with room to store seasonal items such as a jam maker and large pans is important. You'll also need room to store pickles, chutneys and jams, and room for one or more freezers. A cool place to store veg and fruit is helpful too. A large sink area is also desirable and, best of all, a back kitchen with a deep sink and more storage.

A downstairs loo that you can access from outside is essential and the bathroom needs to be in good working order – you'll be getting mucky from the get-go.

You'll also need somewhere for an office to work in and store paperwork and books. If you have a room that can be dedicated to this, it is easier than using a corner of the kitchen or living room.

Home Comforts

Make sure there is an efficient heating system and, if based on wood, make sure that wood is easily available in the area. If you are using solid fuels, there must be somewhere outside to store them and close enough for you to be able to get fuel in during bad weather. If using logs, you'll need a dry log store, close to the house.

Make a list of anything you will want to do to the house in order of importance; so re-roofing comes before redecorating. Get the essentials done in case you run out of money!

Checklist

▶ **Start small:** However much land you have available, begin in a small way and grow.

▶ **Choose to do things you like:** Grow tomatoes if you enjoy salad or keep sheep if that is your interest. Don't do things just because you think you should or because you think they will make money. Things you are interested in are more likely to develop into a business.

▶ **Consider water use wherever you live:** Most experts believe this will be a future issue. Plan your growing with water in mind.

▶ **Land needs:** Be honest about the amount of land available to you.

▶ **Planning permission:** Never ever assume you will get planning permission for anything.

▶ **Works costs:** Cost all renovations and building work inside and out and budget for it.

▶ **Learn and experience:** Take time to learn as much as you can about what you want to do and get practical experience. City farms are invaluable for this.

▶ **Join groups:** Get to know the local area and join in – smallholding clubs, allotment organizations, beekeeping clubs... You'll get support, knowledge and usually the opportunity to share equipment.

▶ **Paid work:** Try not to give up all your day jobs. You will need some form of income, and you cannot assume any from your smallholding until your enterprise is up and running.

Growing on Your Land

Your Greatest Asset

Whether you are going to keep livestock or go in for vegetables or fruit, the considerations relating to the soil do not change. Soil is the most valuable part of your entire smallholding.

Not Simply Soil

The all-important soil that makes up the growing abilities of the land comes in a range of textures from clay to sandy soil. The six main soil types are:

▶ Clay
▶ Sand
▶ Silt
▶ Peat
▶ Chalk
▶ Loam

> *Top Tip*
>
> 'Land, then, is not merely soil; it is a fountain of energy flowing through a circuit of soils, plants, and animals.'
> Aldo Leopold, *A Sand County Almanac* (1949)

All these soils were formed in different ways over thousands of years and are the most valuable asset your smallholding will ever have. Without your soil in good shape, you can grow nothing. As soil cannot be man-made and it takes a thousand years to generate just three centimetres of it, the only thing that can prevent degradation is careful management. Organic farming and permaculture are methods particularly sympathetic to soil, although cultivation methods such as zero-till in commercial growing can also be beneficial.

Clay

Sandy

Silty

Peaty

Chalky

Loamy

Know Your Soil

Firstly, identify which type or, possibly, types of soil you have. This is usually done by soil analysis and is money well spent, particularly when you are starting out.

63

Testing your soil is good practice for various reasons:

▶ To know best **how to care** for it and **manage** it according to the type.

▶ To understand what you will need **equipment**-wise.

▶ **Some crops do not like certain types** of soil and don't grow well on them.

▶ To find out if it **holds water** or not.

▶ To adjust your **stocking rates** according to how well it can maintain grassland.

Clay

Clay soil is what we call 'heavy' land. Anyone who has ever walked across a saturated field in late winter will have worked that one out for themselves, as it clings to boots and even sucks them off. It feels lumpy and very sticky when wet and then goes rock hard when dry, so if it is 'poached' – that is, damaged by livestock trampling it – then the rock-hard lumps just stick up like concrete blocks. The feet of grazing animals can destroy good pasture in a day or two if too many animals graze on soil that is too wet. The advantage with clay is that it holds water and can continue to grow grass during dry weather, unlike sandy or peaty soil.

Sand

Sandy soil is the ultimate in well-drained soil but is not high in nutrients, so requires both feed and water to grow well.

Silt

Silty soil is formed from riverbeds and as such is fertile and light, but is easily compacted by livestock or machinery.

Peat

Peat is very black and is part of fen land. It is just like a giant grow bag – it is very rich, grows everything but dries out quickly and is given to blowing away if hedges are removed.

Chalk

Chalk soils stand up well to livestock, as they drain easily, but they are very alkaline and don't hold water well.

Loamy Soil

Aim for something in the middle, a loam soil that is dark and friable. It is easy to cultivate, retains water and, if attention is paid to putting back what you take out, will provide nutrients too.

Caring For Your Soil

All of the soils have their advantages and disadvantages, and you have to learn to work with them to get the best from them and to give something back to them in the form of organic fertilizer, manure or green manures (plants grown to use as mulch and then dug in to condition the soil). The choice of plants grown in the soil will have an effect on its fertility. Cereals and many root crops will deplete soil fertility, whilst legumes such as clover and peas or beans will capture nitrogen from the air and deposit it in the soil.

Continual mowing, with the removal of the crop for hay or silage, will rapidly deplete soil fertility, whilst grazing and topping (*see* page 68) leave the nutrients in the field. So for hay and silage (known as forage crops) the needs to be managed to get nutritional crops.

Drainage

Soil moisture is essential for plant growth, be it crops or grass, but too much water can be detrimental and drainage of some sort may be necessary. Ditches, to intercept and divert surface water, are relatively cheap and can be very effective. There is also the option of under-drainage, using plastic or clay pipes buried deep in the soil, but this is very expensive and needs careful planning. You can normally tell if the land has been wet even in the summer by looking round the gateways to see if the ground is uneven from the winter.

> **Top Tip**
>
> Learn how to manage your soil and try to keep everything, including yourself, off it when it is wet.

Soil Compaction

This is a problem on all soil types, as heavy machinery and overstocking of animals pack the soil to the point that the minute creatures in the soil that maintain its fertility struggle to survive. Compaction hugely reduces the growing capacity of the soil and stops water being absorbed, causing both flooding and, ironically, lack of moisture in the soil. If you have taken on land that is in good order, plan to avoid compaction. If you have taken on compacted land, you will need to take steps to bring it back to good health. Begin by liming and adding organic matter to encourage earthworms, and move on to aerating or ploughing (or digging) if really bad.

The QMS (Quality Meat Scotland) has a particularly good booklet available online called 'Better Soil and Grassland Management for Scottish Beef and Lamb Producers' – its advice applies to everyone. The Royal Horticultural Society, also online, has good descriptions of soils and how to fix problems.

66

Getting Growing With Grassland

Grass is the green wonder of the smallholding. It is such a good-tempered crop, coming back year after year and responding with enthusiasm to the longer, lighter days. So look after it, care for it and protect it.

Grassland Care

It is much easier to protect grassland than to rebuild it. Stocking rates should be in accordance with the amount of grass, the type and condition of the grass, and the drainage. Never ever overstock – always go lower than suggested stocking rates. Grassland is the most valuable source of cheap and nutritious food for your animals, so value it.

Topping

Perhaps the most delightful feature of grass is that it thrives on being cut or grazed and immediately puts additional effort into growing more aggressively. 'Topping' means cutting at a height of 10–15 centimetres to weaken weeds such as docks, thistles and nettles when they are at their most vigorous and forming seed heads. Do not top poisonous weeds such as ragwort, as livestock will eat them. Remove all poisonous weeds by digging. For organic growers especially, good management and prevention is key, as if the ragwort or grassland weeds are too numerous to dig out manually, you will have to consider spraying to get them under control. This will have to be done by a qualified spraying operator.

Re-seeding

This term is bandied around a lot when grassland looks in poor condition but, in reality, establishing a grass (also known as a ley or sward) is very difficult and takes time. Re-seeding is an absolute last resort, especially if you want to use your grassland within the next couple of years. Try to improve the grass you have. If very weedy, then ploughing will spread the weed seeds and allow them to come back even stronger, so you need to deal with these first or take measures to encourage the grass to outgrow them.

Top Tip

'I believe a leaf of grass is no less than the journey-work of the stars.'

Walt Whitman

If you do go for a re-seed, choose the seed very carefully for your soil type and drainage. It's better to have a mix rather than one type of grass seed and you can incorporate wild flowers and herbs with the mix.

Managing Manure

Horse owners will know of the importance of removing droppings from the paddocks to try to stop the life cycle of worms. With farm animals, a system of rotation and harrowing is used instead. When the grass is grazed down, the animals are moved on to fresh pasture and the droppings are harrowed to be spread all over the grass. The animals are kept off the field for several weeks before being returned and the same thing is done to the next field or paddock.

It is also a time to deal with persistent weeds, cut nettles and remove any poisonous plants. If you have a muck heap it can be spread on to your land, but many areas are now NVZ (Nitrate Vulnerable Zones) and will be subject to restrictions. NVZs are designated areas of land that drain into nitrate-polluted waters, or waters that could become polluted. Check to find out if you are in such a zone.

> 'It's Midsummer Day and they're cutting the hay down in the meadow just over the way.'
> 'Haytime', Irene F. Pawsey

Haytime Is Playtime

Well, not really playtime, but if the weather is right, it is a real relief to get the hay done ready for another winter. Haymaking is quite straightforward; it's the wild card of the weather that makes it tricky.

Conserving Grass

For many smallholders with small numbers of stock, rather than keeping them off the grass until the end of June or early July when the hay can be made, it's going to be more practical to use your grazing for your livestock from early spring (especially if you have lambs planned) and buy in your winter hay supplies. However, if you do have some spare grassland, then you can make your own hay.

There is no fixed time to make hay, especially in our increasingly erratic summers, but some people prefer to leave it until late June so the ground-nesting birds have hatched and the wild flower seeds have spread. Quite edible hay has been made in September. Others prefer to go for an early cut, either to be sure they have it safe or because the food value may be higher.

How Hay Is Made

To make hay, you need either four to five blisteringly hot days, ideally with a light wind, or a week of no rain but no really hot weather. So when the weather forecast is promising and the ground is dry, the hay is cut and lies on the field for a day or so to dry. It is then 'turned' to another position to get it to dry. This is the skill of making hay. A thick crop

A hay baler.

Top Tip

Hay is the safest method of conserving grass, as you can easily tell if it is not right for consumption, as it will be dusty and smell mouldy.

may need turning several times in difficult weather so it is dry and smells sweet. If it rains at this time, all is not lost, but more turning will be required. However, the longer it rains, the more the feed value will drop and continual rain may cause total loss of the crop. It's a very stressful time for the haymaker, as this is the only chance to conserve a year's worth of growing grass.

71

Gathering and Storage

The decision to bale is ideally made when the hay is at the right level of dryness, but sometimes a forecast of heavy rain means it may get baled a bit earlier than it should be. If there is too much moisture in the dried grass, the hay will go mouldy. Amazingly, haymaking is still done largely by eye, nose and common sense rather than by any technical instrumentation, so use your intuition and consider these options:

▶ **Hay:** You can bale hay into large or small bales. Small are much easier to handle but have to be gathered in before it rains, whilst bigger bales can stand a bit longer on the field.

▶ **Silage:** Some dry weather is needed for silage (which is not suitable for equines), contrary to popular belief. The grass is cut and baled when green and damp, and then wrapped to keep out the air. The grass begins to ferment, but as there is no oxygen, the fermentation process is halted. It must be made properly and can be dangerous to stock if not.

▶ **Haylage:** This is a cross between hay and silage. It is left to dry longer than silage and it should have had sun on it, but fermentation still takes place. The air is excluded by wrapping it. It can be fed to horses, but if you have made it from your own grass, it is a good idea to get it tested: some moulds that can enter haylage are highly toxic. Haylage bought from agricultural merchants will be professionally made and usually tested.

Straw

Straw is the by-product of a cereal crop, primarily wheat, barley and oats, though you can get pea straw (goats like this). Smallholders are unlikely to grow these crops, but you can buy it direct from the farmer; be sure to make the arrangements early in the year so that you have some reserved. As with hay, it needs to be baled dry, which can be harder to achieve in the autumn.

Top Tip

Neither silage nor haylage should be regarded as the 'easy option'. Both still need some good weather and are more difficult to make properly than hay, as you'll need plastic and special wrapping machines.

73

Root Crops

If you have some spare land, even just 20 by 20 metres, you could think about growing some fodder beet or mangelwurzels (also known as 'mangold wurzels'). These are fed as part of a balanced diet for ruminants and are much enjoyed. They are chopped or sliced before feeding. They are quite easy to grow; just plant them and keep them roughly weeded. Watch out for potassium deficiency when the leaves become yellow. They like full sun and you need to keep them watered, but they don't like to sit in the wet. Mangelwurzels grow to be several kilos per root. The leaves are edible for humans and taste like an earthy spinach.

Fodder beet or Mangelwurzels are a nutritional feed.

Fodder beet is often described as a cross between a sugar beet and a mangelwurzel. As with mangelwurzels, fodder beet are planted in the spring and lifted in October/ November. The lifted roots must be protected from frost. Those with space might also consider growing turnips, swedes and large varieties of carrots for animal feed.

Tempted by a Tractor?

Do you need a tractor on your smallholding? It depends on the size of your smallholding and what you want to do on it, but for many, the tractor makes the smallholding. There are many uses for a tractor: it can pull, plough, lift, move muck with a bucket and drive post-hole borers.

New or Second-Hand?

A brand-new tractor will give you more reliability and versatility, but at a price! For those who are less confident with mechanics, buying new is a good choice, as you should have the support of the supplier.

If, however, you are mechanically minded, you can make hay on a small acreage of up to 15 acres with an elderly tractor, a turner (such as a 'wuffler' or acrobatic rake), and an old baler. After all, that's what they would have used in the 1950s and '60s – not the huge tractors of today. Here are some points to look out for when buying an older tractor:

▶ **Get advice:** Take someone who knows what they are looking at.

▶ **Test the tractor:** Just as you would when buying a car, check that things such as the hydraulics, steering and brakes work.

▶ **Take a close look:** Appearances can be deceiving – newly painted does not mean a good engine.

New tractors come in various sizes. Check that they can be registered for public road use before you buy. The cheapest may not always be the best, but if price is your main issue, then check you can get spares and that there is a dealership in your area. Be careful, as some of the new tractors don't work so well with older implements, so you may need to budget for these as well. Check with your supplier.

Take time to find out all you can about your choice of tractor so that you can use it to its full potential. There are many tractors, both old and new, that do very little of what they are actually capable of due to their owners' lack of knowledge. Training and advice via your local smallholding club or agricultural college will pay dividends.

Where to Buy a Tractor

For a new tractor, check out the advertising in tractor and smallholding magazines and also look for your local dealerships. Talk to other smallholders too and see what their experiences have been.

For an older tractor, the four main ways of buying are:

▶ Privately
▶ From a dealer

▶ From a farm sale
▶ From a collective sale

77

Private Sales

This could be from another smallholder who is giving up or moving on to another tractor, or from someone who renovates and sells them on. Above all, try the tractor and see it do everything.

From a Dealer

There are highly reputable dealers who will offer a backup service and there are those (not many) who just move machinery on as quickly as possible. If it is your first tractor, try to work with a recommended dealer and tell them what you want and what you want to do with it.

From a Farm Sale

Most farm sales are genuine: the farm may be changing hands or the farmer retiring, and the tractors you are viewing will have worked on the farm up until more or less the time of the sale. However, it's worth checking in the catalogue that the tractors are the property of the farm and not being sold on behalf of another – they may be fine, but it's best to know where they came from. Get a bidding number before the auction starts, decide upon a realistic price to pay and don't go far beyond it. You will also need to arrange transport home for your tractor. Don't expect to get a cheap tractor – everyone else will also be looking for a bargain!

From a Collective Sale

Here, sellers will have brought tractors from all over the country to a central sale. Information will be provided in the catalogue, but you need to find the seller to ask any further questions. Again, take someone knowledgeable about tractors with you and talk to other people looking at the tractors. Collective sales are very friendly and a great day out – it's worth visiting a couple before deciding which tractor you want.

Types of Growing

Choosing the type of grower you want to be is an important decision. You might even say it's an ethical one even. Anyone who's tried to grow fruit or vegetables will know it's not just us humans that enjoy the taste of them. Deterring pests and combatting disease is an ongoing challenge, but there are a variety of approaches to how you meet that challenge.

Conventional Farming

This allows the use of all approved chemicals within a country for both crops and livestock. For many smallholders, their management will include some chemicals, especially to begin with as they learn how to produce food.

Most livestock keepers will usually use chemical wormers, sprays and pour-ons to prevent flies and maggots. Vaccinations will also be used. Chemicals to deal with specific crop problems (such as a major infestation of ragwort) would be acceptable to many, but routine spraying for pests that could be controlled in another way is best avoided; similarly for plant diseases caused by poor or non-existent rotation. The thought of enhancing rather than exhausting the soil is the first principle in any self-sufficiency production and healthy soil will in itself prevent many plant and even livestock problems.

Organic Farming

Organic farming is much more than just not using chemicals. To do that without understanding the principles of organic farming would endanger the welfare of your livestock. Organic farming embraces a whole ethos of working with nature to utilize her ability to produce fertile soil and control pests and diseases in both plants and animals.

Organic farming methods are a huge step towards sustainable agriculture, and organic farmers are expected to have respect for their livestock and the countryside and to abuse neither, providing farm animals with a lifestyle as close to their wild, natural habitat as possible.

For most smallholdings, the cost of registration with one of the organic certification bodies in order to use their logo and describe the produce as 'organic' is too expensive. Groups of smallholders can join together to get certification in some cases. But you can still run your smallholding according to the principles.

Much has been written on how to farm organically and much research has been and is being done, so it is helpful to join organic organizations to get access to this information. Organic farming does not and should not deny welfare treatments to sick animals, nor deny worming when necessary – the idea of organic farming is to prevent such situations arising with non-intensive management.

Permaculture

Permaculture takes organic farmers one step forward, actively working with nature. Permaculture attempts to model its methods on ecosystems, which are natural communities of wild plants and animals, such as forests, meadows and marshes. Mechanization and oil-based fuels have no part to play in permaculture!

The example used by those who promote permaculture is the abundance of growth in forests and woodland, with far greater production per acre than arable or grassland farming and all without any cultivation, weeding or fertilizer, and very little work by man.

There are now recognized courses on permaculture across the world. When planning your smallholding, it may be worth exploring one of these.

Making Your Garden Grow For You

The soil type, the garden situation, the amount of land available, your time and, maybe most importantly, your preferences, will make the smallholding garden personal to you and your family. There is no right or wrong thing to grow – this section identifies some basic ground rules and explores some possibilities to inspire you.

What and Why to Grow

There are so many different crops you can grow, even once you've narrowed it down to those that suit your soil type, so how to choose? You might start by asking yourself why you want to grow:

▶ **To make some money:** The right choice of crops grown on the right sort of soil in the right way can generate a useful income.

▶ **To live the 'good life':** To be self-sufficient or partly self-sufficient in veg and fruit.

▶ **To have a healthy hobby:** To have some homegrown crops that suit your lifestyle and soil.

▶ **To try something new:** To grow fruit and veg that are difficult or expensive to obtain in shops.

Growing For Money

Of all the smallholding activities, growing is the one most likely to provide a profit of some sort. It is hard work, needs excellent marketing and expertise, but the potential for profit on a small scale is there if you are using polytunnels or greenhouses. This is why in the early twentieth century, the smallholding was often structured around the model of the market garden, with livestock important but taking a back seat to the all-important work of the garden. Most of the livestock would be largely consumed by the family with the exception of Christmas poultry and eggs, while the vegetables and fruit would not only feed the family but also be sold for cash along with flowers.

Where is the Value?

Choosing crops to sell means evaluating where you are going to sell them. Then make the choice from things that have more value than mass-produced crops or are a specialist version of something mass-produced, such as heritage or coloured potatoes.

Selling Flowers and Plants

Homegrown cut flowers will have more value than homegrown cut cabbages and can be taken a step further to be used in floristry. The market gardeners of the early twentieth century loved to grow flowers for sale. Pot plants, bedding plants and hanging baskets are all things that are saleable and can add to your offering.

Herbs are mostly easy to grow and are saleable to gardeners or those with window boxes to fill. A knowledge of their uses and advice to buyers will help to sell them.

Festive Crafts

Wreaths at Christmas are always popular and you can grow the foliage as part of your hedges. But what about birthday wreaths, Easter wreaths, new home wreaths or new job, new baby or marriage wreaths? There are numerous occasions where a fresh flower wreath would be popular.

Living the 'Good Life'

To be partly or fully self-sufficient, firstly
you need to work out what you need in
terms of quantity and types. Potatoes
will be your prime concern (and storage
of them) and then other vegetables will
be strictly seasonal. There is a so-called
'hungry gap' in early to late spring,
especially if the brassicas have bolted,
and this is where frozen, bottled or even
pickled vegetables come into their own.
Autumn-sown broad beans may also help.
A polytunnel to increase the length of
growing is an invaluable asset.

A Case-Study for Self-Sufficiency

In the 1940s, when crops yielded a bit less than they do now, it was estimated that a vegetable plot of
250 square metres (300 square yards) would produce enough to feed a small family. More recently, a
crop of summer vegetables worth £262.54 at supermarket prices was harvested from a plot of just 30
square metres (35 square yards) by mail-order seedsman D.T. Brown. The company grew 16 different
varieties from its catalogue, a packet of seed of each, costing £31.46 in total. In many cases, only a
fraction of the contents of the packet was used, so the seed cost could be spread across more than
one year. In the trial, the crops received no special treatment and were picked two or three times a
week, starting on 8 July and ending on 4 October, taking only the best from all the varieties and leaving
anything which was 'past it'. With better planning and more picking, the spread of species grown and
the value of the crops could have been considerably higher.

A Healthy Hobby

It's a practical idea, especially if time is very limited, to grow the crops best suited to your soil and situation and to the time you have available. These will be personal to you but the following work well:

► **Early new potatoes:** These are an exciting and worthwhile crop and taste fabulous homegrown.

► **Tomatoes:** These are a hugely versatile crop and can be grown in tubs, in pots, in grow bags, indoors or outdoors. They come in so many types, from plum to cherry, from garden tomatoes to beef-steak type. There is a tomato for every situation and taste.

► **Lettuce or salad leaves:** The huge choice of varieties in cut-and-come-again leaves means fresh salad is almost always available.

► **Runner beans:** These are not only generous in their produce but are lovely to look at. They are attractive enough to be grown in the border. French beans are also good and are more to some people's taste.

► **Courgettes:** Another generous plant that doesn't mind growing in a small space. Also the obligatory Hallowe'en pumpkins grow easily and generously, and provide a good quantity of vegetable.

► **Spinach:** This can be quite expensive in the shops yet grows rapidly and there is a bi-annual type that is cut-and-come-again.

Trying Something New

This is likely to include heritage varieties of most vegetables where taste rather than quantity is what is needed. Many of these varieties cannot be sold due to laws relating to the sale of seeds, so there are organizations that will swap or take donations for these precious old varieties.

Top Tip

Join your local gardening club. They have helpful talks and demos and often access to a discount on garden products

Also, for example, farmers generally don't want to grow climbing peas, as they need supports and can't be harvested mechanically. Lots of smallholders prefer tall pea varieties, as they are more productive in a small space. There are hundreds of examples like this – the needs of smallholders and farmers are very different. There are also more exotic vegetables that are not readily available in shops or are, like spinach, very perishable and better grown at home.

Getting Growing

There are an ever-increasing number of ways to grow your seeds or plants, but one of your growing needs is mostly out of your hands, and that is the weather. Protecting crops such as by covering with fleece or using a polytunnel or greenhouse can greatly alleviate the effect of bad weather, but not always as much as you might like. The weather will play a big part in growing, and planning ahead for different weather conditions and working with what comes is part of the smallholder's/gardener's life.

Preparing the Ground

First you'll need to clear your veg patch! To do well, you need to prepare well and there are various methods you can use:

▶ **Digging and double-digging:** Digging is usually sufficient, but double-digging (digging up one layer of soil and then loosening a second layer to which compost or other organic matter is added) may be necessary for very poor, heavy or compacted soils, or for certain crops such as asparagus.

▶ **Mechanical rotovation:** You can hire a rotovator or your smallholding club may be able to put you in touch with a member who will lend you one (be sure to replace oil, fuel and any parts that you break).

▶ **Animal rotovation:** Pigs are excellent at turning over soil. Ducks will clear invertebrates and thrive on them.

▶ Black plastic: A layer of this (or old carpets) will stifle weeds, but there may well be seeds left that will germinate.

▶ Chemicals: As a last resort, you may want to consider using a herbicide that will kill all the plants in the area in which you want to grow. Follow instructions carefully and leave time before planting.

Top Tip

Soil can almost always be improved by composting and digging in well-rotted manure.

Raised Beds

This method of growing – where the soil level is raised and contained within a surround, usually of wood but it can be blocks – was first talked about in the 1970s and has revolutionized the way both domestic and commercial gardeners can grow vegetables.

Working with Raised Beds

▶ Make it deep: The bed should be as deep as possible, as it will retain moisture and allow vegetables with deeper roots to thrive. Shallower beds will grow salad crops.

▶ Prepare the soil: Compost should be dug in to enrich the soil.

▶ **Plant close:** Vegetables are spaced so that they just touch each other (you have to decide how big each plant will grow) and this helps to reduce the weeds.

Benefits of Raised Beds

▶ **Soil quality:** In some countries, this technique means that poor soil can be improved with composting rather than having to plant into dry, poor conditions. This can apply to anyone anywhere in the world whose soil is not very productive, and is very handy if you want to grow some crops while you are improving your veg plot.

▶ **No compaction:** The gardener does not walk on the beds, so there is no soil compaction, which can hinder growth.

▶ **Ease of access:** Anyone with a back problem or in a wheelchair is able to tend their own garden, and it is easier to use protective fleece or covering to keep out eager beaks and mouths!

All the above means there is much more control over the growing, and raised beds generally result in higher yields for a small area and make larger plots more manageable.

Growing in Small Spaces

There are some inventive ways to make the best use of small areas or, indeed, to create small productive gardens in dry climates:

▶ **Square-metre/foot gardening:** A bed is divided into equal squares and each square planted with a different vegetable, so that there is always something to pick and eat throughout the growing season.

▶ **Vertical growing:** This is where you grow in baskets and containers up high rather than on the ground. A lettuce really doesn't care if it's six foot off the ground, as long as it has its water and nutrients. It means you can use wall space and is great for people who find it uncomfortable to bend.

▶ **Keyhole gardens:** Originally used in Africa, these are a round raised bed a metre or so in height with a path to the centre so you can tend it all without walking on it. In the centre is a 'compost well' that retains water and nutrients and allows them to feed out to the surrounding garden in a controlled fashion.

▶ **Bag gardens:** Based on a similar idea to keyhole gardens, these make the most of soil, compost and water. By growing in a bag, you keep out weeds and other soil contaminants, and retain moisture. Drainage is provided by holes at the bottom and, in the case of typical vertical African bag gardens, building in a vertical drain in the centre out of stones.

91

The Organic Option

For many smallholders, growing organically is the ultimate aim. Permaculture and organic growing were discussed on pages 80–81 of this book and both can be practised in the garden. At the very least, smallholders will want to work with nature and can do this using a number of techniques that avoid the overuse of chemicals.

▶ **Physical barriers:** Netting fruit and veg will usually avoid the need to spray for pests.

▶ **Companion planting:** This is where plants that repel certain insects are situated next to those that attract them and helps to reduce or eliminate chemical control.

▶ **Choice of varieties:** There are so many available that you can select those that are disease-resistant.

▶ **Manage your expectations:** Be realistic about the success of a crop – if you lose a crop to caterpillars and you don't want to use chemicals or kill the caterpillars, then change the crop to one less prone to attack. Some crops simply are not worth the effort involved to protect them.

▶ **Manual removal:** This is the disposal of pests by natural methods such as squashing them rather than spraying.

▶ **Biological control:** This uses other organisms that rely on predation, parasitism, herbivory or other natural mechanisms, but also involves active human management.

▶ **Rotation:** Moving your crops and growing them in different locations from year to year reduces pests and diseases. More on this below.

Each type of crop takes different amounts of nutrients from the soil, and legumes even give something back. Different crops attract different pests. Therefore if you grow each group of vegetables in a different situation every year, you can rotate them so that there is not a buildup of pests or diseases and the soil is not drained of a particular nutrient. These groups are:

▶ **Root vegetables:** As the name suggests, these are vegetables where you eat the roots, such as beetroot, carrots, parsnips; they are often grouped with alliums, such as onions.

▶ **Brassicas:** These include Brussels sprouts, cabbages, cauliflowers, kale and other green leafy veg but also radishes, swedes and turnips.

▶ **Legumes:** These include broad beans and peas. French and runner beans, although legumes, are less susceptible to disease and pests and can normally be grown anywhere. Runner beans will have had a bed prepared with a thick layer of organic mulch under their roots.

▶ **Potatoes:** These are sometimes included with root vegetables, but they are a family of their own which includes tomatoes and peppers.

Rotation means alternating each vegetable from a group, so that if you choose to have a four-fold rotation, you might grow potatoes the first year, legumes in the same spot the second year, then root vegetables and finally brassicas.

The marigold is a classic companion plant, as it can protect tomatoes from whitefly and can lure aphids away from beans, as well as attracting some beneficial insects.

Crop Rotation

Root vegetables

Brassicas

Legumes

Potatoes

Protected Cropping

All serious smallholder gardens need a greenhouse. Even a modest three metres by two metres will provide an excellent start to a range of seeds, and will grow tomatoes, peppers and cucumbers for the house. Situate it where the sun can get to it and where you can easily reach it with water.

In some areas, polytunnels will require planning permission and more likely to do so if for commercial use. They require careful situating, with the long side running from east to west and, of course, with consideration given to the wind in exposed areas. It is best to consult with the manufacturers to get the best advice.

Top Tip

This is not a complete guide to growing fruit and vegetables. For more specific information on growing food, refer to titles such as our *Grow Your Own Vegetables* and *Crops in Pots* by Rachelle Strauss.

Creating an Orchard

Traditional orchards, once a common sight in the countryside, have declined by nearly 60 per cent since the 1950s. Smallholders can play their part in planting new orchards to take their place and managing them in an eco-friendly way.

For the Time-Short Smallholder

For the smallholders among you who have to combine full-time and demanding jobs with your love of self-sufficiency and fresh food, an orchard is the perfect way to make the most of what you have in the time available. Unlike livestock, it doesn't need attention every single day and you can plan the picking for top fruit (tree fruits).

> 'Even if I knew that tomorrow the world would go to pieces, I would still plant my apple tree.'
> Martin Luther

Apples and Other Top Fruits

Apple trees are the basis of an orchard and there are hundreds to choose from; there's even a special toffee apple variety – Cockitt's Red! If you contact your local heritage orchard stockists or association, you'll get a wealth of help and advice on the individual varieties.

Apples are grouped into early, mid-season and late, and you can plan your cropping from this. They are further divided by how long they will keep if correctly stored. Also consider the pollination group; if the tree is not self-pollinating, you will need a tree of the same pollination group to set the apples. There are so many varieties that you can plan enough to keep you in apples from August to May – August for the early fruiters and May for apples that will store. Choose the apple for your purpose such as culinary, dessert, dual-purpose and cider. Don't forget to plant some nut trees too.

Conditions to Consider

▶ **Think about drainage:** Fruit trees will grow in an incredibly wide range of soils but do not like being waterlogged. For a traditional orchard, do not attempt to 'improve' the soil but in a back garden or allotment, the trees can benefit from mulching with organic matter.

▶ **Plan your access:** At harvest time you'll need to pick the fruit and get it out of the orchard, so allow more rather than less space around the apple trees. Think about how you will manage the grass around the trees.

The small, fast-growing hazel tree is an ideal nut tree for the smallholder.

▶ **Offer protection from the wind:** You'll need a natural windbreak around the orchard in the form of a hedge – willow will grow obligingly quickly and provide material for willow weaving. Otherwise native hedging is slower-growing but can provide foraging opportunities for both you and wildlife. You might also consider plums or damson trees, which are more wind tolerant.

▶ **Consider the available light:** Cooking apples and Morello cherries are more tolerant to shade (this is because acid tasting fruit don't need so much sunlight to develop sugar).

▶ **Be aware of frost pockets:** These can be an issue in undulating ground. This is not a problem in winter but when the blossom is on the tree it will devastate the crop. The solution is to choose taller trees and late-flowering varieties.

Top Tip

'You could make an apple pie everyday for 16 or more years and not use the same variety twice.'
Common Ground, *The Apple Source Book* (1991)

Caring for the Orchard

It's important to learn how to correctly prune
trees, especially in their early years. The
grass and other plants must not be allowed to
'strangle' the young trees. The grass needs
to be either cut or grazed. Most animals will
eat trees as well as grass, especially young trees. More established orchards can be grazed by geese
and sheep – the Shropshire is a perfect orchard sheep. Browsers like goats are death to orchards and
any trees near larger livestock such as horses and ponies need fencing off.

The orchard is a
great place for
wildlife and will
encourage fungi,
lichens, plants,
insects, birds and
mammals, and
you might even
be lucky enough
to establish some
mistletoe. As an
enterprise, you
might want to
plant some holly
varieties for
winter wreaths.

Working with Wildlife

It is a good idea from any number of points of view to support biodiversity on your smallholding, but the fundamental interdependence of all living things in this world makes it natural that we should protect them in order to ensure the sustainability of our lifestyle and productivity.

Keep a Record

The first step in improving conditions for wildlife on your smallholding is to identify your existing wildlife by careful observation. Keep a notebook of the birds you see, the insects and mammals, and learn to identify them. It's a great idea to keep a wildlife calendar. noting the weather and any sightings.

Make a Happy Habitat

All birds and wildlife need somewhere to breed, shelter and food. Here are a few ways in which you can make life a little easier for nature's little helpers:

100

March

25 Monday
Rain a.m. sunny p.m.
Twenty-three sparrows on food station
Pair of wrens courting   Hare in lower field

26 Tuesday

27 Wednesday

28 Thursday

29 Friday

30 Saturday

31 Sunday

British Summer Time begins
Mothering Sunday (UK, Eire)

▶ **Don't be too tidy:** Leave cover for insects and small mammals, especially in winter. If possible, have some shrubs or a hedge for birds to perch and nest. Leave some deadwood logs for beetles. Ivy is especially good, providing late-autumn nectar for insects (and honey bees) and shelter and fruit for birds. (If you have livestock, ivy should be kept away from them.) Hedges and shrubs should not be trimmed during the nesting season from April to the end of July, and even outside these months watch out for second broods. Keep a small patch of long grass to encourage insects for the birds.

▶ **Consider having a bird feeding station:** Remember to regularly and thoroughly wash the containers. This is because where birds gather together, they are more likely to pass on disease. In heavy rain or frosts especially, put out some food for the birds, as they will struggle to find it on their own.

▶ **Water features and ponds:** These are great for wildlife and are used by birds for drinking and for bathing, while ponds encourage aquatic insects, dragonflies, frogs and toads to breed.

▶ **Go easy on the slug pellets:** Look for alternative methods, of which there are many, from copper rings to crushed eggshells or a tobacco solution. If you really have to use pellets, check the label very carefully for safety and remember that birds will eat the slugs that you have poisoned and you need to be sure that this will not harm them.

Top Tip

Learn to love slugs and snails. They are food for so many creatures, from small mammals, toads and larger mammals such as urban foxes to the fast-disappearing song thrush.

101

Getting the Buzz

Bees are well known to gardeners and a real sign of summer. Their contented droning as they busy themselves about their work of collecting nectar is sweet music to gardeners' ears; the pollen the bees spread in their passing is crucial to helping the garden grow. The more bees the better! Sadly, their numbers are down. This is due to the loss of many traditional farming habitats and they are thought to be directly harmed by the use of agricultural pesticides, though now these are much more tightly controlled.

Be a Friend to Bees

Bees are such a boon that the grower would be well advised to do as much as they can to attract as many as they can. Here are just a few things you can do:

▶ **Give them their favourite food:** Bees get the most nectar from traditional cottage-garden flowers and the least from annual bedding plants such as pelargonium, begonia and busy lizzies. In early spring, your fruit trees, such as apple, cherry, pear and plum, will attract them and then, in early summer, they enjoy thyme and chives (plus flowers such as wall flower, campanula, honeysuckle and single roses). In the late summer, they love lavender, mint and marjoram, and are very attracted to sunflowers.

▶ **Give them a good home:** Providing a bee-friendly habitat on your smallholding can help, both the bees and your crops. Bumblebees like a dry, dark, ventilated cavity with a small entrance hole they can access at ground level. They like a sheltered spot along a hedge or fence out of direct sunlight. If you don't want to create your own, you can buy purpose-built bumblebee nests.

The Tree Bumblebee prefers to nest above ground and so may make use of old bird boxes.

Can I Be a Beekeeper?

One sure-fire way of helping pollination is to keep honeybees. However, keeping honeybees needs care and specialist knowledge, so before you decide whether you could be a beekeeper, ask yourself some questions:

▶ Can I cope with having buzzing, stinging insects in close proximity even with a safety suit?

▶ Can I site my hives (more than one is known as an apiary) in a safe place?

▶ Can I attend a beekeepers' course locally and join a bee club?

▶ Am I good at carpentry? (It's not essential, but very handy for making up frames.)

Top Tip

There are between 10,000 and 60,000 bees in a hive and helping them to stay alive and well is a huge responsibility.

Siting the Apiary

This needs to be in a completely safe place that children and animals cannot access. You cannot site hives in a field with livestock unless they are very well fenced off. Bees fly upwards, so a high fence will encourage them to go above neighbouring gardens and your property.

The apiary also needs to be accessible, as hives are heavy and you need to be able to get a wheelbarrow into the site. You will also need to feed the bees in the winter and at times of low food supply.

You will need a water source, as the first thing bees need to do in the spring is to drink. If there is no natural source, you'll need to provide a source with sides that bees can grip.

Choosing a Hive

There are two ways of keeping bees. One is purely as pollinators so you can use a top-bar hive or similar design, but more usually they are kept for honey. If you choose the latter, there is a choice of hives, the most usual being the National hive in the UK or the Langstroth hive in the USA, for example. If you buy second-hand hives, they must be scorched to kill disease and fitted with new frames.

Buying Bees

If you have joined a bee club, then they will help you get a colony of bees with a good temperament. If not, you will have to try to buy from a local beekeeper, who will also act as your mentor.

Buying Equipment

You will need a full-face veil and a suit that can be tucked into wellies and gloves. If there is an area of you that is unprotected, the bees will find it! In addition, you'll need to buy and know how to use a smoker.

A National hive.

Inspections

Inspections are done to check the following:

▶ **Is there enough room for the brood nest and for honey storage?** This is particularly important early in the year, to reduce swarming, and during a honey flow. 'Super' boxes are added to a hive to give bees somewhere to store their honey.

▶ **Are eggs, larvae and sealed brood present?** Seeing eggs tells you the queen was there at least three days ago.

▶ **Is the colony size as expected?** In the spring, the number of frames with brood will be increasing. After the colony peaks, they will reduce as the bees get ready for winter.

105

▶ **Are there occupied queen cells?** This means the colony is preparing to swarm and control measures need to be implemented.

▶ **Are there signs of disease?** Some diseases can only be identified under the microscope, but the state of the colony will alert you to their possible presence.

▶ **Is there enough food?** If not, you need to feed the bees.

Honey Harvest

Honey is taken when there is sufficient for you to take some and for the bees to still have supplies. You will need to have a honey spinner on which you fix the frames and turn them by hand or by motor to extract the honey.

Alternative Ways to Help

Having considered what is involved, maybe beekeeping is not for you. That does not mean that you cannot do your bit to help the bees. One of the problems they face is a reduction in suitable forage and you can help counteract that by planting bee-friendly flowers in your garden, especially those that flower in spring and autumn. This will really help make a difference to the survival of bees of all kinds.

Top Tip

For a comprehensive guide to beekeeping, refer to our companion title *Keeping Bees*, by Pam Gregory and Claire Waring.

Checklist

▶ **Look after the grass:** Grassland is your best friend – take good care of it. Don't poison your stock – check your grassland for poisonous plants.

▶ **Soil:** They don't make it any more, so nurture what you have. Know your soil type so you can work with it.

▶ **Do you need a tractor?** Choose the right one for your smallholding.

▶ **Make hay:** Haymaking is for everyone, as long as you have the right equipment and weather.

▶ **What type of grower are you?** Are you conventional, organic or permaculture? Know the different types of land management. Grow with nature in mind. If you're not going organic, then reduce or eliminate chemical use by your choice of growing methods.

▶ **Get the best from your crops:** Prepare your veg patch before sowing or growing, understand and practise crop rotation and consider protected cropping.

▶ **Prepare for honey bees:** Join a bee club, go on a course and get a bee mentor. Choose your bees carefully for temperament.

▶ **Get a good start for your bees:** Be sure that your bees are sited in a safe place for you, your family and your livestock. Watch out for disease – start with clean hives.

Sourcing

Livestock

Preparing to Source

The housing is ready, the runs are secure and the paddocks are well fenced. Now is the time to start to look for your new arrivals, but where do you start? Sourcing good stock is a skill that you need to learn.

Know What You Want

Websites, social media, local sale sites, newspapers and magazines and the recommendations of friends – these are all potential sources when looking for animals for sale, and we'll discuss these a little more later. But the choices can be overwhelming and just how accurate are the descriptions? It is very important before beginning to source stock to know exactly what you want. It's a bit like taking a shopping list to a supermarket: if you stick to it, you spend what you've budgeted for and don't come out with something that is no use to you. These decisions will be guided by:

► Experience
► Space
► Time
► The end product

Experience

It's always a good idea if at least one of you knows what you are doing! If your end product is to be goats' milk, then it may be an idea to source goats that have some idea of what's required. Clearly, before getting a dairy goat, you will have learned how to milk and care for them, but to begin with, you will want to look for a dairy goat who has kidded successfully and been in milk and milked for a couple of years. They (for you must have more than one) won't be the cheapest way of getting started, but the experience you'll get will pay dividends in that they will be used to being milked.

If buying poultry for eggs for the first time, don't start with chicks, as these require specialized rearing and equipment. Start with a POL (Point of Lay) hybrid hen who, if properly managed, will lay an egg a day for around 300 days of the year.

Top Tip
Know your ideal stocking rate and understock rather than overstock.

111

Despite their small size, Soay sheep need space to range.

Top Tip

The higher the stocking level of livestock, the more management, and therefore time and expertise, they will need.

Space

Across the many breeds of both livestock and poultry, there are obvious choices according to the amount of space available. Confusingly though, it's not all about the size of the breed, though that's very important. Some breeds, like the diminutive Soay sheep, simply cannot tolerate small spaces, as they are what is known as 'primitive' breeds and need space to range. Other, larger sheep are more domesticated and, although they need to be able to graze, they can cope in an orchard or smaller paddock.

However, generally speaking, the larger the breed, the more space they need. Large fowl, especially those with feathered legs or a profusion of soft feathers on their bodies, need plenty of space. Most 'off-the-shelf' poultry houses are too small for them – they need room to stretch up and flap their wings. The doors (sometimes called pop-holes) into the houses need to be big enough so the hens don't have to stoop and won't catch themselves on them. They also have large feet that paddle small areas into mud when wet, so they need a larger area to keep them content.

Time

Be brutally honest about how much time you will have. The time taken will be reduced by having very good facilities; so half a dozen laying hens in a large, fox-proofed run and well-designed house will be easier to care for than birds in a pen that is falling to bits. Hard standing (paving slabs or concrete) around animal housing makes it even easier, as does lighting. Poultry houses need to be easy to clean so you can access everything inside without twisting your body – being able to stand up in them makes it easier still. Money and time spent setting up good facilities will pay you back over the years in time and the resulting health of the livestock.

If keeping cattle, you'll need to have handling facilities where they can be confined safely and pens in the field for catching, as without these, you'll find the simplest task not only more time-consuming but also more dangerous.

Timber Flair's 20 Bird Pent is large and easily accessible.

113

Livestock require daily care and additionally there are seasonal tasks. For poultry, for example, you'll need to factor in red mite prevention; for sheep, there is dagging (removal of dirty wool around the back end), as well as shearing, vaccinations, hoof trimming and prevention of fly strike. You can't go on holiday in April/May without having treated them for fly strike and shearing must be done when the weather turns warm.

The End Product

So why are you keeping the poultry or livestock? If you want to fill your few acres with field animals that are pets, don't let anyone put you off as it is your choice and your money. If they are for the freezer or to provide fibre, milk or, in the case of poultry, eggs, be sure you select the right stock.

For pets, you'll want non-breeding animals and poultry – hens don't need a cockerel to lay eggs and cockerels will happily live together in groups if you don't have any females about and they have sufficient space to range. Field animals such as sheep and goats can be wethers – this means they are neutered at an early age and will be easier to handle than entire males. Larger animals such as donkeys and horses should always be gelded unless you have a very clear breeding purpose for them, otherwise they'll have a miserable life of frustration.

Selecting stock for production must be based on getting the best example of that breed that you can. Some sheep, cattle and goat breeds (such as the Boer goat) are specialist meat breeds, so do your research. In poultry, the ultimate layer is the hybrid hen and/or ex-battery hen. Then there are the dual-purpose breeds, which produce a reasonable amount of meat and milk or, in the case of chickens, a reasonable carcass for cooking and a respectable number of eggs. Light Sussex, Rhode Island Red and Wyandotte chickens were originally bred to fulfil this function, but now you have to ensure you get a laying strain rather than an exhibition bird (*see* page 117).

The Boer goat is a meat breed.

It costs as much to keep a poor example of a breed as a good example, so look for the best you can afford.

Breed the Best

Buying livestock to breed requires careful consideration. A single ram may be responsible for producing half the flock – that means his characteristics will come through all the ewes to their lambs. If you use a substandard ram, you will not produce the standard of meat or breeding stock that you want. That's why seriously high prices are paid for seriously good rams. You probably won't be able to afford the very best, but you get the best you can afford. If you can't afford a good male, consider hiring in or using artificial insemination if appropriate to the type of animal. Producing top-class stock means you can ask top-class prices for the offspring.

Pick the Right Cockerel

Similarly with poultry, it's important to buy the best if you are intending to breed. Hybrids are proven layers, but if you are buying a pure breed such as one of those mentioned above, the cockerel must come from a 'laying strain'. This means his mother was a good layer and she will have passed on her genes to him and he will pass them on to the flock. In the 1930s, breeders could command the equivalent of a thousand pounds for a cockerel from a hen that had laid 300 eggs in two successive seasons, by a cockerel whose own mother also had an excellent laying record. These days, you won't ask or get anything near that sort of money, but it's worth paying the premium if a breeder can verify the laying record.

Up to Standard

Particularly with poultry, some sellers make inaccurate claims about their birds, so you need to have in your mind what sort of characteristics the breed should have to help you spot anything that is not up to standard. The most commonly misrepresented is the Aylesbury duck – not every large white duck is an Aylesbury. If it has a bright orange bill, it isn't a true Aylesbury but a commercial breed. That's not to say that the lower-quality birds are not delightful and good layers, but you won't be able to breed top-quality stock with them. Commercial white geese are often described as Embden, and sometimes Roman if they are smaller, and their prices inflated. Commercial breeds of geese are still lovely to keep, lay well and are good for the table, but you should be paying less for them than a pure breed and you should be aware that you won't get the pure-breed premium for their offspring.

The Aylesbury duck breed is not to be confused with generic commercial breeds.

117

Which Breed?

Pure breed, rare breed, cross breed or unknown? All of these have their advantages and disadvantages and all have their place, but which one is for you?

Pure Breeds

Apart from poultry, pure breeds are only such if they are registered with their breed society. Never ever buy a so-called pure breed with the hope you can later register it. Most societies have strict rules about registering and will require a lot of confirmation of identification. Just because it looks like a breed does not mean that it can be registered, and if it can't be registered, then neither can its offspring.

The Advantages

The obvious advantage of buying a pure breed is that you know what you are getting. Many years of breeding have meant

The Saanen goat is a pure breed developed for its milk.

the characteristics are defined, such as colour and markings, but more importantly, so are production qualities such as milk and meat. The Saanen goat, for example, through years and years of selecting the highest milkers with the largest udders, is an outstanding dairy goat and good examples well kept will reliably produce an expected amount of milk.

Even temperament can be predicted in pure breeds. Pigs with floppy ears, such as the Gloucester Old Spot and Large Black, are supposedly more placid than other breeds. In poultry, the Mediterranean breeds such as the Ancona, Leghorn (which used to be a major laying breed) and the Minorca are undoubtedly 'flighty' – that is less placid and more inclined to being reactive. When you buy one of these breeds, you know what to expect – don't open the carrying case without them being secure in the pen!

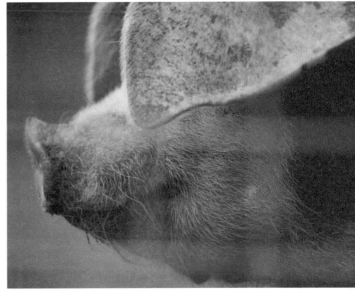

But Beware

But across all breeds, although the looks, markings and production may be predicted, there is often a difference in an individual's temperament. So although there is an indication in each breed, don't completely rely on the animal or bird behaving in that way. The trick is to also breed for temperament as well as the other characteristics, and by careful selection, you can do this.

The Gloucester Old Spot pig is a placid breed.

119

The Bagot goat is a rare breed.

Rare Breeds

These represent a way to preserve the past for use in the future. The rare breeds of today were often the popular breeds of the past, bred for a specific reason to meet the needs of the population at the time. Tastes change, farming methods change and the once-popular animal finds itself without any demand and therefore is not bred or kept.

Yet most have helped shape the human race in one way or another: their history is also our history and their future is important to our future. For example, the trend for intensive pig keeping has now been joined by a return to outdoor pig keeping on a commercial scale, which means the new breeds need hardiness. Where better to find this gene than from the breeds of the past? Conservation grazing has meant there is a new demand for the Bagot goat, while Shropshire sheep, who prefer to graze rather than browse, have found a new use in orchards.

What Are Rare Breeds?

Rare-breed farm animals and poultry are recognized in most countries by the low

120

numbers of breeding females and are brought together by organizations working to keep them, and therefore their gene pool, alive.

Organizations exist around the world to support rare breeds: the Rare Breeds Survival Trust in Britain, the American Livestock Breeds Conservancy in the USA, the Rare Breeds Conservation Society in New Zealand, the Rare Breeds Trust of Australia, and Rare Breeds Canada, plus organizations in most European countries. These organizations work together exchanging knowledge, and the endangered stock they are concerned with represents stock indigenous to their country as well as stock bred for purpose.

The Clun Forest sheep is a cross breed with Shropshire sheep in its mix.

Cross Breeds

Although occasionally unplanned, cross breeds are more usually created for a purpose. For example, using a Boer goat on a dairy goat means that the resulting kids will produce more meat.

121

A 'terminal' sire in sheep is a ram that is a different breed from your ewes. It is used to produce cross breeds with traits that are better than the animals you started with, in particular meat production and finished weight for slaughter, hence the name.

Hybrid hens are a form of cross breed in that various poultry breeds were carefully selected to bring together the best characteristics in one bird. The desirable hybrid characteristics might be purely in terms of egg laying, such as a hen destined for intensive farming; or the

The Leghorn played a significant role in the breeding of hybrid chickens (a form of highly cross bred chicken).

aim might be to produce a better layer than a pure breed but with additional hardiness; or another hybrid might be developed with a certain egg colour in mind.

Unknown Breeding

Finally, we're including poultry and animals of unknown breeding. They will still lay, produce meat and happily live as pets, but if you breed from them, you will not easily sell the offspring as breeding stock. You can improve this by using a quality pure breed, which may help in terms of dairy or meat but will still make the chickens an unknown breed and therefore of less value. That's not to say they cannot be attractive and are, of course, unique. They are also cheaper to buy.

122

Breeds in Brief

There are hundreds of breeds of livestock and new ones being introduced every year, so this is not a complete list but some of the main ones that would be commonplace in smallholding.

Chickens

The traditional way to begin poultry keeping is to buy Point of Lays (POLs). These will be hybrids at between 17–20 weeks of age just about to start laying eggs.

Top Tip

Always buy your POLs at the same time, as introducing new chickens to established ones can be difficult and cause stress.

An alternative could be year-old birds that have been in intensive farming, known as ex-batts. They still have plenty of laying life, but need special care to adapt to a free-range life.

Pure Breed Parade

There are many varieties of pure breed hens, from bantams to large fowl. Not all are good layers, some are very decorative but not productive, and all have been bred for a particular purpose such as egg laying, for the table or purely for their looks.

Aesthetics versus Productivity

Generally speaking, those that lay the really wonderfully coloured deep brown eggs, such as the **Welsummer** and the **Maran**, lay less often than the white-egg laying Mediterranean breeds, the

The Welsummer chicken.

The Rhode Island Red chicken.

The Wyandotte chicken ('Golden Pencilled').

Leghorn and **Minorca**. The much-loved **Buff Orpington** is a very large bird that needs a good-size hen house but lays a comparatively small egg, and these days is not the best layer. The **Rhode Island Red** and **Light Sussex**, despite now being bred more for the exhibition bench, do retain some of their utility characteristics by providing a good-size carcass and some strains lay a reasonable number of eggs (150–225 a year). **Wyandottes** are also kept as dual-purpose birds.

Need to Know Gender?

There are also the auto-sexing breeds where you can tell the sex of the chicks by their colour, such as the **Cream Legbar**.

Rare Breeds

For the more adventurous, there are the rare breeds, such as the magnificent but large **Jersey Giant** that was bred solely

Top Tip

For a more extensive range of chicken breeds, check out our companion title *Keeping Chickens*, also by Liz Wright.

KEEPING Chickens LIZ WRIGHT

for meat production. The Poultry Club of Great Britain has a good list of all the breeds on their website with their full descriptions and it's well worth visiting a poultry show and having a good look. Bear in mind that heavily feathered breeds need dry conditions and may not look too good walking round a muddy smallholding!

Bantams

Chickens are categorized as large fowl (breeds like Rhode Island Reds). Many of the large fowl breeds have miniature versions, which are commonly known as bantams. They don't usually have the laying record of their larger relations.

True bantams are breeds where there is no large fowl counterpart, such as **Pekins**, **Belgian Bantams**, **Japanese** and **Sebrights**. Bantams such as Pekins are ideal for children as they are docile and attractive. The **Silkie**, with its remarkable feathers that have led them to being described as 'chickens with fur', is not only ornamental but has an advantage when it comes to incubating eggs. The **Serema**, recently introduced to the UK, is the smallest bantam and is ideal as a pet.

The Jersey Giant table chicken.

The Pekin – a true bantam chicken.

125

The Indian Runner duck (white).

Ducks

All domestic ducks are descendants of the wild mallard except the **Muscovy** duck, which is a South American tree duck. Categories for ducks are:

▶ **Call** (they are noisy but very cute)
▶ Bantam and miniature
▶ Light duck
▶ Heavy duck

The Indian Runner

This outstanding egg-laying breed came to the UK in the nineteenth century. Producing around 200 eggs a year, it prefers to range and forage over a large area. Classed as a light duck, it can be quite jumpy, but these days cannot fly.

Call Duck

This is the archetypal 'rubber duck' with round body and head, alert eyes and small bill, this small bird makes a large noise.

Aylesbury Duck

Once the leading meat breed in Britain, finding a true Aylesbury with flesh-coloured bill and blue eyes these days is quite a challenge. It is a placid breed that does not fly.

The Call duck (white).

126

Appleyard and Khaki Campbell

These ducks astounded people when they were developed in the early part of the twentieth century for their outstanding egg-laying ability whilst providing a useful carcass.

Muscovy

Large distinctive ducks that hiss and, as such, are sometimes mistaken for geese. They lay very well, are exceptionally hardy and excellent parents as well as producing good carcasses. But they are the Marmite duck – you either love them or hate them.

Commercial Duck

Developed from the pure-breed ducks, there are several commercial types, most deriving from Pekins for meat, but some developed from the Khaki Campbell for egg laying. White ducks with orange bills are commercial types, not Aylesburys.

The Appleyard duck (female) – the standard colour is Silver.

The Muscovy duck.

127

Geese

Geese are available as light, medium and heavy breeds. All domestic geese are descendants of the **Greylag** goose, except the **Chinese** goose and the impressive **African** goose.

Well-known goose breeds seen on the smallholding include the **Roman** goose and the noisy **Chinese** goose, which is often kept to warn of visitors. The **Embden** is a large white goose, often confused with the white commercial goose. The **Toulouse** is a heavy goose and is almost stately as it moves. It can get fly strike in its loose feathering. The **Pilgrim** and **West of England** geese are both auto-sexing, so you can tell the sexes from their colours as small goslings.

No one really keeps geese for their eggs, as the heavy breeds tend to lay around 25 eggs a year, the commercial breeds about 60, with the Chinese goose being the best egg layer at 60–100 a year. Most breeds have been developed for meat or feathers, with the Chinese having the additional reputation as a guard goose.

The African goose.

The Roman goose (tufted).

The Pilgrim goose (female).

Turkeys

The turkey is one of the most efficient meat-producing animals in the world, so it is easy to see why it is so popular. Commercial varieties mature at around five months of age, with the standard rare turkeys taking a few weeks longer. They can therefore provide a seasonal income within six months, provided there is a market for your product.

The Norfolk Black turkey.

Incubate or Eat

The turkey is a seasonal layer, producing 50–70 eggs a year throughout spring and summer. If hen (female) turkeys are running with a stag (male), then the eggs will be fertile and able to be incubated to produce your own poults. Should you have a glut of eggs, or wish to keep hen turkeys only and thus only have infertile eggs, the eggs can be used or sold for eating. Turkey eggs are extremely good to bake with, as the abundant albumen is wonderful for soufflés and sponges and the creamy yolks make thick pastry sauces. Two or three females will provide eating eggs throughout the season.

The Bourbon Red turkey.

Breeds

Turkey breeds include the influential **Norfolk Black** and the **Bronze**, both of which are kept on smallholdings for the Christmas table. Commercial varieties are often white and are also used for Christmas. Exhibition breeds, such as the **Royal Pam** and **Bourbon Red**, are kept for their beauty. The **Narragansett** is believed to have descended from a cross between wild turkeys and the Norfolk Black, with the **Slate** turkey also deriving from the Norfolk Black. Although these birds are usually ornamental, surplus stock will still make a good meal.

The Narragansett turkey.

129

Other Poultry

There are other birds worth considering:

▶ **Guinea fowl:** These produce good meat whilst ranging, but can take it into their heads to fly away. If penned, they need considerably more space than chickens.

▶ **Peafowl:** Normally kept for their beauty, although if they breed, peafowl can command a good price. Need a lot of space and ideally to range.

▶ **Quail:** Diminutive birds that are good layers. They also can be eaten. They need special care if being bred, as males will over-mate and have been known to injure females.

The Japanese quail.

The Toggenburg goat.

Goats

One of the most productive and versatile animals on the planet, the goat is best known for its ability to produce milk.

Milk Goats

Dairy breeds include the highly productive **Saanen**, which may produce too much milk for the average family. The **Toggenburg**, the **British Alpine** and the **Anglo Nubian** are all impressive milkers but not quite in the league of the Saanen. The **Golden Guernsey**, which is a smaller breed, is often kept

131

The Anglo Nubian goat.

The Angora goat.

as the smallholding goat, as it produces enough milk for a family (and probably some to spare), is easy to handle due to its size, and generally has a very placid temperament.

Not Just Milk

Goats also produce meat and fibre, and can be pets or driving goats (goat carts were popular in the 1920s and 1930s and usually pulled by a neutered male of the larger dairy breeds). As well as milk, goats are kept for:

▶ **Meat:** The **Boer** is the go-to meat goat and, with its distinctive red and white coat pattern, is also lovely to look at.

▶ **Fibre:** The **Angora** is a fibre goat with a lustrous fleece and is great for home spinners. The **Cashmere** is also a fibre goat, but is smaller and not kept as much.

▶ **Pets:** The outstanding pet goat is the **Pygmy**, which is charming and friendly, although it is best to neuter the males if not needed for breeding.

▶ **Land management:** Finally, the **Bagot** deserves a mention, as it now has a place as a conservation grazer on large estates.

132

Sheep

Keeping small numbers of sheep and especially rare-breed sheep is popular amongst smallholders, as they provide meat for the freezer and fleeces for home spinning. Sheep milking has also enjoyed an increased following. Sheep need good grass in plentiful supply: if you don't have this, don't keep sheep.

An Adaptive Animal

Areas throughout the world have developed sheep that have adapted to thrive in particular conditions, with perhaps the most extreme example being the seaweed-eating **North Ronaldsay** from the Orkneys. Broadly speaking, sheep can be divided into four categories: the long-woolled breeds, once prized for their fleeces but with many now featuring in the rare-breed category; the short-woolled, which tends to include a lot of lowland breeds that have been commercially successful as they are more 'meaty'; the mountain breeds, which have adapted to very independent living on rough grazing; and the primitive breeds, which are the ancient sheep breeds and are leggy, small and active. There are also some breeds of sheep developed for dairying.

Long-Woolled Breeds

These include the **Wensleydale**, which is a very large sheep that produces a fleece of outstanding quality and quantity. Because of its size, it's not ideal for beginners. The **Border Leicester** is another large sheep, white in colour, which produces a

The Wensleydale sheep.

The Greyface Dartmoor sheep.

The Merino sheep.

heavy, good-grade fleece, as does the **Teeswater**. The **Dartmoor** is a moorland sheep that likes extensive conditions and produces a long, curly, lustrous wool of good quality. The **Lincoln Longwool** is the largest of all, with the heaviest, longest and most lustrous fleece, ideal for hand spinners. They are docile but large! The **Merino** is an economically influential breed that is prized worldwide for its wool.

The Hampshire Down sheep.

The Suffolk sheep.

Merinos are regarded as having the finest and softest wool of any sheep. All long-woolled breeds produce a slow-maturing, large and lean carcass, but the emphasis was historically on their wool, leaving meatier breeds to take over when the demand for wool decreased.

Short-Woolled Breeds

These include most of the lowland and downland breeds. They are smaller and stockier, with good-sized limbs for producing family-size joints. These include the black-faced **Oxford Down**, **Hampshire Down** and **Dorset Down** (also useful as a dairying breed) as well as the **Southdown** (of which there is a miniature variety, which look like teddy bears!). All breeds are renowned for being placid and early books talk about them being ideal for 'the lady shepherdess'! The similarly placid **Suffolk** grows to a large, commercially meaty carcass. It is known for early maturity, but may require more supervision during lambing than the

Shetland sheep come in a variety of shades.

The Badger Face Welsh Mountain sheep (Torddu pattern).

independent upland breeds. All lowland breeds require good-quality grass in order to fulfil their meaty carcasses.

Upland and Mountain Breeds

The **Welsh Mountain** is a survivor, able to live in the most testing conditions, as is the diminutive **Shetland**. Both

The Herdwick sheep.

breeds are small and, although lively, are therefore relatively easy to handle. The fleeces are good for hand-spinners, with the Shetland coming in a number of colours. The **Badger Face Welsh Mountain** comes in two varieties: mainly white (Torddu) and mainly black (Torwen). The **Exmoor Horn** is a white-woolled, hardy breed, a good producer on lower ground, but also able to live well on moorland and rough grazing. The **Herdwick**'s fleece was once in huge demand for carpets, but is now more valued for its carcass of dark, fine-grained meat from low-value, fibrous grazing.

Primitive Breeds

Keepers of these claim a well-flavoured meat, but the carcass will be small and take time to mature. They are remarkably hardy, but can be difficult to domesticate. Their fleeces can be rather sparse, yet are highly valued by home spinners. They are nearly always horned, with the **Hebridean** and the **Manx Loghtan** being multi-horned (sometimes even growing up to six horns). Difficult to categorize, the distinctive black and white **Jacob** is kept for its lovely coloured wool, its longevity, its lean but slightly gamey meat, and its striking looks.

The Jacob sheep.

135

The Wiltshire Horn sheep.

Dorset-Friesland cross milking lambs.

The North of England Mule sheep (produced from a Bluefaced Leicester ram crossed with a Swaledale or a Northumberland-type Blackface ewe).

Other Specialist Breeds

The **Wiltshire Horn** is a large, white-faced breed that produces good carcasses but naturally loses its wool without shearing, saving on costs where the wool is not required. It is a placid breed.

The **British Milk** and the **Friesland** have been developed for milk production and have the ability to produce more than twice the yield compared with other breeds. The Friesland produces milk with a high butterfat content for up to 10 months of the year. The **Dorset Down**, unlike other breeds, has the ability to produce three lamb crops (litters) in two years if well managed and well fed, and is sometimes used as a dairy animal as a result (because you get three lots of milk in two years).

Commercial Sheep

If a hardy hill ewe is crossed with a long-woolled ram, then it will produce a half-breed. The resulting ewes are then crossed with a terminal sire, a breed that stamps fast growth of a meaty carcass on the stock to produce meat lambs for the market. So if selecting purely for the freezer, consider a commercial breed. Perhaps the best-known of these are the 'mule' cross breeds, which are created from various crosses: for example, the **Scottish Mule** that is the progeny of the Blackfaced ewe and the Bluefaced Leicester ram. Rearing a couple of orphan lambs from a commercial farmer is a good way to start producing meat for the freezer if you have sufficient time and an excellent way to prepare for breeding your own sheep.

Alpacas and Llamas

Alpacas and llamas come under the umbrella of camelids, a category that also includes guanacos and vicuñas. They all originate in South America, but only the llama and alpaca have been truly domesticated and are found worldwide. Kept for its luxury fibre, the alpaca was bred from the vicuña, a smaller camelid which has the finest natural fibre in the world. The llama, larger and more chunky than an alpaca and bred from the guanaco, can produce a rough sort of fibre, but is best known as a pack animal.

There are two main types of alpaca – the **Huacaya** and the **Suri**. They are easily distinguishable and what you keep is down to personal preference. The 'teddy bear' Huacaya with its dense, crimped fibre is the most popular around the world. The Suri has a silky coat which hangs down in long ringlets. Equally there are two types of llama – the **Ccara** (larger, with shorter hair) and the **Tampuli** (more heavily woolled).

The Huacaya alpaca.

From Fleeces to Fun

So why keep alpacas and llamas? For their fleeces, as guards for poultry and smaller animals, for breeding (be sure you invest in the best breeding stock you can), but also because they are fun to keep and great for therapy and as pets. You can take your alpaca to shows and also show their fleece. There are an increasing number of people enjoying trekking or walks with their llamas. Alpaca agility is also a new leisure pastime (they love a challenge!) and alpacas as therapy animals are also proving successful.

Get Advice

Organizations such as The British Llama Society (BLS) and the British Alpaca Society (BAS) or the Alpaca Owners and Breeders Association (AOBA) in the US, for example, exist to support members and promote

137

The Ccara llama.

> ## Top Tip
>
> Alpacas and llamas are naturally herd animals and must never be kept on their own. Keep at least two, but ideally more.

these camelids. Anyone keeping either species is urged to join the appropriate breed society. The societies operate a pedigree register and it is very strongly recommended that only registered animals be purchased. Advice and assistance, particularly with welfare issues, is available from each society.

You can access the details of breeders from the societies. Prices will vary according to the quality of fleece of the alpaca and the sex. A female with a high-quality fleece will be very expensive, as she will produce stock with high-quality fibre and they will be valuable. A highly graded stud male will also command a high price. But if you want them as pets or to access fibre for home spinning, you could look for neutered males or those animals with lower-quality fleece.

Spin Out the Benefits

Due to careful breeding since their importation, even the lower-quality fleeces are good for home spinning, especially when learning. It is worth taking time to learn what makes a high-quality fleece, and many alpaca studs offer training days for would-be buyers and courses for anyone interested. Smallholders who get the most from their alpacas are those who are skilled at spinning and working with fibre. It can be costly to get small amounts of fibre spun so, for small numbers of alpacas, it is advisable to spin the fleece yourself. There is a limited market for hand-spun yarn, so any money is really in finished items such as shawls, scarves, socks and garments.

138

Pigs

Most smallholders start by buying piglets, either of pure breeds or commercial breeds, and bringing them on to slaughter weight either as a porker, cutter or baconer, depending on their breed.

Weights

Weights and ages of the different product types tend to be as follows*:

Finisher Type	Product Required	Average Liveweight (kg)	Average Age (Months)
Porkers	Pork	60–75	4–5
Cutters	Pork and Bacon	76–85	5–6
Baconers	Bacon and Ham	86–110	7–8

Top Tip

Generally speaking, pigs with snub noses such as the Middle White prefer to graze, while longer-snouted pigs prefer rooting.

*Source: Meat Promotion Wales.

The Tamworth pig.

Breeds

Smallholders often keep rare-breed pigs or the more traditional breeds that are hardy and thrive outside. The **Gloucester Old Spot** is generally good-natured, while the **Large Black** is another good-tempered pig that is ideal for keeping outside. The **Saddleback** breeds were traditionally hardy, while the **Tamworth**, with its long snout, is an excellent forager and is often used to clear land. The **Oxford Sandy and Black** is another docile pig that is a good converter of food to weight. The **Berkshire**, black with white feet, is hardy, but is more of a porker than a baconer.

A Berkshire piglet.

If looking for pet pigs, the friendly **Kunekune** is popular (though, despite being small, they can and do grow quite large enough to be a useful meat pig). **Vietnamese Pot Bellied** pigs, with their appealing wrinkled faces and intelligence, can become very much part of the family (their meat, though valued in the Far East, is not usually to Western tastes).

Cattle

Cows, being ruminants, require grass as a major part of their diet, so need a large area of grassland. When no fresh grass is available, they enjoy silage, haylage or hay, and will eat small amounts of straw to help their digestion.

A good way to gain experience is to buy 'store cattle' in the spring. These are around two years old and are then simply 'finished' – that is, brought up to slaughter weight by the smallholder. Calf rearing is also a good way to start, but needs skill, knowledge and experience in selecting the calves.

The 'house cow' (that is, a cow kept to provide milk just for you) really will produce vast quantities of milk and, if she is placid, it may be best for her to rear her calf as well as you milking her. If you are a beginner, choose a cow that has already been handled in this way.

Milkers

A dual-purpose breed, which was indigenous to your area a hundred years ago, would be ideal. The **Gloucester** cow, for example, is a compact animal that has been domesticated for generations. Generally speaking, the more traditional breeds tend to be more docile and smaller.

The Ayrshire cattle breed.

The Jersey cattle breed.

141

The **Shorthorn** is a milky and very hardy breed that was once the choice for the dairy industry. The **Ayrshire** was renowned for being exceptionally hardy and a good milker. England's East Anglia produced the **Red Poll**, a hornless breed, which is a good mother. The **Jersey** is the ultimate dairy animal, producing milk that is high in butterfat.

The little dual-purpose **Dexter** is a favourite amongst smallholders for its size, but it can be

The Dexter cattle breed.

The Hereford cattle breed.

quick tempered and should be handled with respect despite its diminutive size.

Best for Beef

Although beef cattle are less suited to milk production, it does not mean that you cannot milk them for your family if they are docile. Known for its distinctive white face, its motherliness and its hardiness, the **Hereford** is a great choice for the suckler herd. From Scotland, the **Aberdeen Angus** is famous for its early-maturing, prime marbled beef. It passes on the polling (non-horned) gene to cross-bred offspring.

Procuring Livestock

Just as you had to take time choosing the best location for your smallholding, assessing the options and asking the right questions, so too must you exercise caution when buying livestock and bringing them home.

Buying Livestock

Here are some of the ways in which you can source livestock and poultry:

Direct from the Breeder

This is by far the best way to buy, so you can see the animals for yourself as well as the parents and other siblings. You can expect a breeder to have pride in their stock and they ought to be able to give you advice on management.

The Classifieds

There are many advertisements in magazines and farming papers and also online. Always visit the livestock, taking a knowledgeable friend if possible. You want to get an idea of how they have been kept and see for yourself their health status and whether they are a good example of their breed.

At the Market

Buying from markets is a very traditional way of buying, however you do need to know what you are doing and what you are looking at. It's a good place to buy, say, store lambs (that is, lambs that are yet to be fattened). With poultry, be sure that the birds for sale are the best example of their type. There are markets that also have grading – where the poultry is given a mark or an assessment. They tend to have the better stock and you can see what you are buying. If buying any livestock from a market, be sure you can quarantine the animals away from other stock for at least a week – longer if possible (as you should for any livestock, but it is especially important for livestock from a market, as they will have mixed with other animals while there). All livestock should be treated for worms and external parasites unless there is clear evidence this has been done. Allow them to settle in for 24–48 hours before doing this to avoid stress.

144

Online

We buy everything online these days, so why not livestock? However, as these are living creatures, additional care needs to be taken. Many people buying direct from a website without visiting have had bad experiences. Websites are fabulous for sourcing livestock and can give you an idea of what to expect, but you still need to visit.

Top Tip

Always view all livestock and poultry in the flesh. Don't buy from a description or photos, unless from a recommended breeder.

From a Charity

This largely applies to ex-battery hens, but some farm animals are also available from charities. Do not expect to be allowed to breed or slaughter them. The charity should give you plenty of information on how to care for your animals and will want to know how you are going to keep them.

Other Sources

When looking for poultry, you might want to consider garden centres (of the larger variety) and specialist poultry suppliers. Usually, hybrid poultry are exactly as they are described but, again, with the pure breeds, it is nearly always better to go to a breeder. If not, you must really know the breed standards before buying.

The exception to the rule on seeing stock is when buying day-olds or hybrids from a specialist poultry supplier. There are some excellent suppliers who can be found in poultry and smallholding magazines and the poultry will be delivered to your door.

Size up the Seller

Someone selling you animals should be able to tell you everything you want to know, should not look impatient with your questions, should ask where the animals are going and how you are going to care for them. If someone doesn't seem to want to answer your questions, walk away. They should be full of enthusiasm and want the best for the animal or birds' welfare, and certainly not want to get rid of you as quickly as possible. Always get a phone number and always get a written bill of sale. If you are in any doubt, don't buy, and if you come across poor animal or bird welfare, report it to the appropriate agency.

Bringing Them Home

Always make sure you have the requisite documents and licences required in your country or state. In the UK, for all farm animals, you will need your agricultural holding number and a movement licence. If someone tries to put a goat in the back of your car without asking to see these, don't buy. There are strict rules about transporting farm livestock – just because you can fit it into the car doesn't mean it is legal.

Appropriate Vehicles and Containers

You will need a livestock trailer with appropriate bedding and which is safe – for example, nothing tied up with string – or you will need a livestock lorry. If you don't have these, you'll need to arrange a friend (try your local smallholding club) or livestock haulier to collect.

For poultry, you will need a box that is large enough to accommodate them and allows them to breathe. Ensure the box is safe so they cannot escape and make sure there is a good airflow. Do not put them in the boot of your car.

Considerate Driving

For all livestock, whether you have them in a trailer or car, drive carefully and think ahead. No sudden stops, no sharp right-hand turns and take roundabouts slowly. Keep the journey time to a minimum – don't stop on the way home for a break unless you are absolutely sure the animals are cool and not stressed. Travelling is a huge stress for animals and poultry, so buy food and water for yourself before you set out and don't stop unless it is a very long journey or you become tired. Plan, plan and plan your journey, avoid rush hour and, if possible, the heat of the day in summer.

Home Sweet Home

More planning should have been done before the new stock arrives. The pen or barn where they are to live should be ready for them to go into immediately. If you have made an 'impulse buy', then you need to plan where they are going quickly and ready the space.

Time to Settle In

They need to get out of the transport and have time to relax, drink and eat. They need quiet, so don't let friends and family do more than just look at them for a few minutes on arrival. Make sure they have everything they need – enough bedding, water containers, feeders and feed, and then leave them. After an hour or so, check to see if they have settled and then top up water and feed, and leave them again.

147

In Sight of Others

It would be a very unusual situation for you to buy a single bird or animal, but if you have, it will be more stressed, so will benefit from being able to see or hear other stock, but remember, there shouldn't be direct contact for a week or so.

Ensure Health and Happiness

Make sure you have the vet's number handy, as well as the number of the breeder or supplier. You might want to contact your smallholding club, too, for advice. If they don't eat, show signs of pain or discomfort, or are particularly distressed and unable to settle, you will need to call a vet. These animals or birds are now your responsibility and their wellbeing is in your hands.

Over the next few days, get to know them and let them get to know you. Be quiet around them and keep dogs and anything noisy away from them. Poultry like treats, such as their corn feed or even some mealworms, and you can soon make friends this way. Friendly animals such as goats like human contact and scratches. Field animals like to be in a field, where they can display their natural behaviour, but make sure you have planned how you will catch them if you need to, for example, handling pens or a supply of hurdles.

And now you are a proper smallholder!

Checklist

▶ **Know what you want:** Decide exactly what you want from your livestock and thus what animals to buy, and how many you want to buy, according to your facilities.

▶ **Do not overstock:** More animals require more management, time and expertise.

▶ **Understand pure breeds:** If buying pure breeds, be sure you know the breed characteristics.

▶ **Let the buyer beware:** Always see the stock for yourself.

▶ **Research the sources:** Don't go for the first source you find.

▶ **Comply with the law:** Have the appropriate paperwork, if applicable.

▶ **Travel with care:** Aim to get straight home, with consideration for the stock in your care.

▶ **Plan the accommodation:** Prepare the pen or barn in advance.

▶ **On arrival:** Ensure they have feed, water and bedding and leave them to recover – keep a quiet eye on them.

▶ **Gradual familiarization:** Get to know your new acquisitions quietly and take it steadily.

Keeping Livestock

Getting the Best From Your Livestock

To have healthy, happy and productive livestock, it is necessary to put a lot into them in terms of knowledge, skill and time. In addition, correct housing with plenty of space, good pasture and the right feed are all good investments in your stock.

The Five Freedoms

Everyone who keeps livestock should be aware of and observe the five freedoms, as defined by the Farm Animal Welfare Council (FAWC) and set out below. The FAWC states that:

'The welfare of an animal includes its physical and mental state and we consider that good animal welfare implies both fitness and a sense of wellbeing. Any animal kept by man must, at least, be protected from unnecessary suffering. We believe that an animal's welfare, whether on farm, in transit, at market or at a place of slaughter should be considered in terms of 'five freedoms'. These freedoms define ideal states rather than standards for acceptable welfare. They form a logical and comprehensive framework for analysis of welfare within any system together with the steps and compromises necessary to safeguard and improve welfare within the proper constraints of an effective livestock industry.'

1. **Freedom from hunger and thirst:** By ready access to fresh water and a diet to maintain full health and vigour.

2. **Freedom from discomfort:** By providing an appropriate environment, including shelter and a comfortable resting area.

3. **Freedom from pain, injury or disease:** By prevention or rapid diagnosis and treatment.

4. **Freedom to express normal behaviour:** By providing sufficient space, proper facilities and company of the animal's own kind.

5. **Freedom from fear and distress:** By ensuring conditions and treatment that avoid mental suffering.

Stockmanship

The FAWC have also established guidelines for good 'stockmanship'. This term is usually defined as the proper handling of cattle, but can be extended to the proper treatment of any farm animal. Stockmanship comes down to the keeper having a thorough understanding of the animals' welfare needs, and ensuring they have adequate training and supervision to competently care for their stock.

So it is important that before keeping any livestock that the keeper finds out how to manage and handle the animal by a mixture of practical and theoretical training and experience.

Are You Legal?

Wherever you are, there are certain legal requirements that must be adhered to. In the UK, for example, before you move any goats, sheep, cattle or pigs on to your holding, you will need a County Parish Holding number (CPH) – *see* page 36. You will also need to register with your local Animal Health Office, who will give you a unique Defra flock/herd mark. All movements will need to be logged

on a movement licence (AML1). Your stock will also need to be identified. The regulations are subject to change, so keep yourself up to date and check on the Defra website. All flock keepers must also keep a flock record.

Keeping Poultry and Keeping Them Well

Poultry are mostly easy to look after, often highly entertaining and, depending on the birds you choose to keep, provide delicious eggs every day. But for all that they give, you need to make sure you can provide them with what they need to be happy and healthy.

The Origins of the Chicken

Gallus domesticus (your friendly chicken) is descended from the Gallus gallus, a bird that is still living untamed in much of South East Asia, where it is known as red junglefowl. There are records of this bird existing some 8,000 years ago. Because the domestic chicken has its wild ancestor still present, it is possible to compare the behaviours of the domestic and wild birds.

Innate Behaviour

Careful breeding has produced hundreds of variations, but even the carefully bred hybrid still retains some junglefowl characteristics! She likes to scratch, sending clods of earth through the air as she looks for invertebrates. Given the chance, she will kill and eat mice and other small rodents. She socializes with others of her kind, and she still retires to a 'safe' place to brood her eggs. She is fearful of large predators and, to her, the family dog is as terrifying as a tiger would have been to her ancestors.

> ### Did You Know?
>
> A hen does not need a cockerel to lay eggs.

The Needs of the Chicken

Knowing her origins, how can we best provide good care for her? She needs:

- ▶ **Safety from perceived predators:** This includes domestic dogs and also over-enthusiastic children.

- ▶ **A safe house:** Somewhere she can perch at night.

- ▶ **A large run:** Where she can express her natural behaviour and, if free-range, protection from foxes and other predators.

- ▶ **A quiet corner:** Somewhere in the dark away from others to lay her eggs.

▶ **Something to drink:** She needs a constant supply of clean water.

▶ **Something to eat:** This should be nutrition that is balanced to her needs: wheat, corn and scraps are not enough.

▶ **Others of her own kind:** But remember the pecking order; don't mix new hens with old without preparation.

▶ **Healthcare:** Management to prevent health problems, but quick intervention if she becomes ill.

Getting Ready for Poultry Keeping

Before the birds arrive, you will need to have a poultry house and run. There are a number of designs for poultry houses, but the basic requirements are:

▶ **Safe and secure:** A safe space in which the birds can be shut at night and where predators cannot touch them.

The Lenham Chicken Coop is designed to be suitable for up to 12 chickens, or for large fowl.

157

▶ **Dry and free from draughts:** However, the space should still be well ventilated.

▶ **With perches:** As most hens like to perch at night.

▶ **With nest boxes:** These should be in a dark and secluded part of the house; some houses have them attached to the side of the house.

Omlet's plastic chicken houses, such as the Eglu, are easy to clean. (Don't forget that chickens who live in houses this small will need a decent-size run in addition.)

▶ **With a clean and dry floor:** A basic necessity for your birds' welfare.

▶ **Easy to clean:** Make sure that the poultry house is easy for you to clean and you can reach every bit of it. Poultry houses are usually wooden and can harbour red mite. If you cannot get to all of the interior, you will never be able to get rid of the mite.

Top Tip

There are now some strong plastic houses that are much less likely to have mite and are easy to clean.

Run Requirements

Poultry houses can be specially made with or without runs. You can use your existing buildings, as long as you remember the golden rules above. A disused stable, garage or a well-made garden shed will all serve well and have the added advantage that you can stand up in them to clean them out.

Poultry runs must be large enough for the birds. Just because five birds can squash into them, it doesn't mean that it is a five-bird run. Hens will forage a considerable distance, so a run needs to be as large as you can make it whether it is four birds or 40. They also need different heights within the run, such as perches or logs, so the shyer birds can get out of the way. Provide 'toys' such as hanging veg – swede or Brussels sprouts for example.

As a rough guide, you need three square metres per hen for the run and a square metre for the house – as they will only be in that at night. More space is always better. The triangular-shaped runs mean that birds have even less space, as they cannot stand up properly along the sides as they slope inwards.

159

A typical feeder.   A typical drinker.

Feeders and Drinkers

There are many of these available to buy, but the most important factor is to provide more than one of each, as otherwise the pecking order means that shyer birds won't get enough to eat and drink. Even if you only have four birds, provide a couple of smaller feeders and drinkers. Not only is this a welfare issue for the birds, but they cannot lay without sufficient water and food.

Ducks, Geese and Turkeys

All of the above applies, except you will need more of a shed-like structure. These birds don't usually use nest boxes, but supply plenty of clean bedding and maybe a corner that is slightly screened off to encourage them to lay.

They are much bigger birds, so will need double the space in a run and double the height so they can stand up fully. Turkeys will need a perch.

Always Water

The big difference for ducks is that they must have water. They need to get their heads right under the water, otherwise they will get eye infections, and they need swimming water to be able to refresh their preening glands. For most sizes of ducks, a hard plastic paddling-pool-type structure of around a metre wide will provide enough water. It will need cleaning out daily, as they defecate in it and the area around it gets very wet as they splash, so you will need a surface that drains well. They also need to be able to get into and out of it, so may need a slope or step.

Geese also need water to completely submerge their heads and necks. Muscovy ducks, which were originally tree ducks, will need a perch.

Daily Care

Each and every day, you will need to check on your birds, ensuring they're watered and fed, and their accommodation is as it should be. However, as happy, healthy birds greet their keepers so enthusiastically, it can be an enjoyable part of your day rather than a chore.

Morning Checklist

Open up the house doors, check the water is clean and feed a balanced pellet according to the type and use of poultry. Briefly check all the birds over. Does anyone remain in the house? They may be laying. Each morning, you should check your birds for the following:

▶ Alertness

▶ **Bright eyes** with no discharge

▶ **Red comb**

▶ **Comb and wattles** should **not be damaged**

▶ **Feathers** should be **tidy and in good condition**

▶ **Feathers** should **not be missing** (except in the moult)

▶ The **vent should be clean** and not be soiled with droppings

▶ **Legs should be clean** and the chicken should not be lame

▶ There should be **no discharge from the nostrils**

▶ The birds should be **eagerly looking for food**

Birds should have healthy eyes.

Before You Leave

If you are out to work for the day, ensure they are left in a large, secure run, safe from foxes or loose dogs. Possibly hang up a cabbage or cut a swede or parsnip for some extra interest. If you are at home, then collect the eggs about lunchtime and check there is sufficient food in the feeder.

In the Evening

Just before dusk, check the birds are still well, and as soon as they have gone into their house, shut the doors up safely. If you cannot get home until after dark, arrange for someone else to shut them in for you, or buy an automatic pop-hole closer which works on a sensor.

On your return to the house at night, the crop (a sac in the chicken's neck which holds food before it travels further down into the gut) should be visibly full (as a bulge at the front of the mid-neck).

The Generous Goat

Provider of milk, fibre and meat, the goat gives much, but requires considerable commitment from the keeper. The average goat lives between 12 and 16 years and it's not kind to keep a solitary goat. But kept well, your little herd of goats will reward you handsomely for your care.

How Much Space Do Goats Need?

Goats must always be kept at least in pairs, as they are herd animals and will be unhappy on their own. These days, goats are not normally tethered as, unless you monitor them all day, it is an unsatisfactory management method with danger to the animal. Therefore, you need sufficient space for them to have a fenced area around their house or a separate enclosure with a shelter.

They are browsers rather than grazers, so they thrive on woody fibre – tree bark, leaves and branches. You can bring them

163

cut branches, just make sure that you don't disturb birds' nests in summer and that the branches are non-poisonous. They like to climb as they do in the wild, so some strong platforms they can climb on, natural mounds or even a strong box will give them great pleasure.

Goat Security

Fencing is of the utmost importance as goats are great escapologists and always want to be the other side of wherever they happen to be.

They can squeeze through gaps, get down on their knees and wriggle under fences, plus clamber or jump over lower fences. Ideally, fencing should be close-set post-and-rail at least a metre and a half in height, perhaps lined with wire sheep netting (but not if your goats have horns). Electric fencing inside the outer fence can also be effective and there is a wealth of fencing to choose from – check with your supplier. Again, don't use netting on horned goats. If the battery goes flat they will simply walk through it, as they will constantly try the fence.

As mentioned above, tethering is the last resort, and if done, needs a proper swivel collar and chain and constant vigilance to see they are not hanging themselves. They need access to water all day; this is especially important if they are producing milk, as this requires considerable intake of liquid, so make sure the container doesn't tip over.

Goat Accommodation

The house needs to be draught-proof but airy and, as with the fencing, it needs to be well built. Goats need to be able to see out of the building, as they are intelligent and interested in their surroundings. A stable or other outside building can easily be adapted, or use a well-

built shed. Pens need to be at least 1.5 metres by 2 metres for a single milker or two goatlings. Light will be needed. The building needs to be on hard standing and have hard standing round the entrance.

Storing and Serving Food and Water

You can partition off a store (be really careful the goats cannot get at the feed) and also an area for the milking stand.

Hayracks are best designed with a lid and put high enough so the goats cannot get in or on them. Water buckets will need fixing with a ring or clip. Ensure that all bolts are goat-proof – they are very good at finding ways out.

Top Tip

It is generally thought that goats can and will eat anything and everything. This is not true and to stay healthy they need to have the right diet. They will also need a mineral block – check it is suitable for goats, as some are not.

Daily Care

In the morning, check the goats over and let them out of the house into their paddock. They should:

▶ Be **bright** and **alert**.

▶ Have no signs of nasal or eye **discharge**.

▶ Produce **firm droppings** that break into small balls.

▶ Be **keen to eat**.

▶ **Not be rubbing**, and with no sign of **wounds**.

▶ Be able to **move freely**, and not be lame.

Nutrition

Goats will need a good supply of fibrous food, such as hay. They also like Lucerne haylage and, if you can find it, clean pea straw. You can cut branches for extra interest, but make sure they are not poisonous and it is not illegal to cut them. In addition, especially if your goats are in milk, they need a balanced ration, which can be bought ready mixed in a bag. There is a special Pygmy mix available as well as general goat mixes and dairy goat mix. Choose the one appropriate for your goats' needs.

Goats need a mineral lick to ensure good health.

Bedding

They should be bedded on fresh straw, which is regularly mucked out, especially when wet. The waste can be composted for the garden.

167

The Small Flock Sheep Keeper

Sheep are especially useful on a smallholding: they keep the grass neater than a lawnmower could and, unlike horses and cattle, they will not break the sod up with their feet. In return, you will get meat, fibre and even milk.

How Much Space Do Sheep Need?

Sheep do require grass and space, so they are not the ideal animal in a small area. Stocking rates range from five to 10 per acre, but it won't support them all year round – grass virtually stops growing in winter. Always understock. Pasture is best left ungrazed for a month or more, depending on the weather and time of year, so aim to rotate your grazing. If you only have an acre, keep only half the sheep allowed for an acre and graze them on half the paddock so you can rotate to the other half to offer fresh grass.

Sheep Accommodation

Housing is only necessary if lambing, and then the building will need to be large enough to take individual pens constructed with sheep hurdles, which are about two metres long. It also needs to be well ventilated. A sheep shelter in the form of a basic structure with a roof and a back, but otherwise open and airy, will help a lot in the cold or wet weather.

Sheep benefit from a place to shelter from sun and storm.

Sheep Security

Well-erected sheep netting that has been correctly tensioned with a post-top rail is ideal. Electric sheep fencing can be used and there are some very good designs, but the fencing unit must always be switched on and working efficiently. Sheep in full fleece find it comparatively easy to push out of electric fencing, so it's best to contain them within a safe outer fence. Don't use electric sheep netting if they are horned.

Nutrition

Growing good grassland is so important for sheep nutrition as it constitutes such a major part of their diet. However, challenging weather patterns can produce a summer where the grass grows profusely after heavy rainfall and an autumn where it shrivels away due to lack of rain. Don't look at the calendar; look at the grazing and feed accordingly. Most small-scale sheep keepers will also need to give supplementary feed for part of the year, and sheep need clean water at all times and a suitable mineral lick.

Top Tip

If mixing types of animals, such as grazing sheep with donkeys or ponies, make sure that the mineral lick is all right for both species, as some contain copper that is fine for sheep but bad for equines.

Extra Nutrition at Key Times

Sheep will also need compound foods that provide protein, minerals and vitamins, plus more nutrition before being put in lamb (tupping), when carrying lambs and usually when being 'finished' for the

freezer. If you have really good grass, you may be able to do this without supplements, but again, it depends on the quality of the grazing available. Lambs are usually given a 'creep' feed to give them a good start.

Daily Shepherding

Always walk round your sheep, preferably first thing in the morning and in the evening before it is dark. They should respond to you, as you will often be feeding them, and they should look interested and alert.

▶ **Are they well?** Watch out for loose droppings and any sheep that are not eating or are hunched up.

▶ **Are they injured?** Sadly, dog attacks are all too common, so check for injuries. It is important to make sure no sheep is lame. Apart from the suffering, being lame will reduce their food intake, which in turn will make them ill.

▶ **Are they fed?** Note the length and state of the grass, and if you do feed them, if they have eaten up the food you have given them.

The Shepherd's Calendar

Sheep are hardy, healthy creatures if given the right conditions for their breed. It's down to you to provide these. They require your care and attention all year round and, at some times of year, all round the clock. Here are the major annual tasks:

Shearing

Sheep must be sheared as soon as the weather heats up, so any time from May onwards, again, depending on the weather. They will suffer if shorn too early and, if the weather changes, be prepared to provide additional shelter. However, they will really suffer if the fleece is not removed in the hot weather. Be sure you have a shearer ready to shear a couple of months before they need doing. Your local smallholding group will be able to help with phone numbers and recommendations.

171

Vaccinations

They will need regular vaccinations and worming as advised by your livestock vet. In due course, you will be able to administer these yourself, but it's important to learn how to do this properly, as you could cause abscesses or put the vaccination into the wrong part of the sheep.

Fly strike is a condition caused by flies laying eggs that hatch into maggots, which then devour the sheep from the inside out. The sheep must have preventative treatments throughout the summer. Don't do it by the calendar, do it by the weather. It could be hot and humid in March, causing the flies to make an early appearance; equally, it could still be warm enough for them in October. Be a weather watcher!

Lambing

This requires extra skills, so invest your time and money in a lambing course. Smallholding clubs, livestock vets or agricultural colleges will often offer these and they are well worth the money. Plan your lambing so that it is at a convenient time of the year for you, such as early spring when the weather is lighter and warmer. You can usually borrow a ram locally rather than keep one yourself.

Interlocking sheep hurdles.

There's a lot to lambing, so shadow a shepherd and get as much knowledge as you can before you lamb your own sheep. Above all, allow plenty of time to check them – you'll need to do this round the clock – so book time off work. It's proven that early intervention will save many lambs' and ewes' lives and this comes from good observation. Every death should be carefully considered for why it happened and lessons learnt.

Handling and Containing

For all of the above tasks, you'll need to be adept at handling your sheep. Buy at least a dozen well-made sheep hurdles so you can erect catching pens and 'races' – that's where you make a track from hurdles to lead the sheep into the pen and then pull the hurdle across to contain them.

Top Tip

Get your sheep as tame as you can and get them to come to a bucket. It makes handling much easier.

Pig Keeping

Cottagers used to say that you could use everything from the pig but its squeak! But pigs can also be pets and provide companionship. Pigs can help in the garden too – they provide manure and are delighted to help you turn over rough ground. Pigs, if well kept, are clean and easy to look after.

Accommodation

Pigs are strong animals and can be hard to handle. The housing needs to be able to stand up to digging, rooting, and pushing and shoving. There are some excellent pig houses ('arks') on the market but they will need a strong fence around them. You could convert a brick-built outbuilding but it needs to have good ventilation. It helps with the smell: even if kept very clean, pigs have a pungent smell!

Somewhere to Root

Pigs like to root, so it is important to set aside an area for them to use, bearing in mind they will devastate it. You might be able to use this to your advantage, and the turned over area could be used for growing. Although pigs were often kept in sties in back gardens, these days, keeping pigs in a confined area with near neighbours is not satisfactory.

Top Tip

A rubber water bucket clipped to the wall should solve the problem of having the pigs break it during rough play.

175

Somewhere to Keep Cool

Pigs need shelter in the hot sun and ideally a wallow. Provide plenty of straw for the bed and the pigs will be much cleaner, though you will still need to muck them out regularly.

Feeding Time

This should be fun both for you and the pigs. They need to be fed at least twice a day and to be able to look for food for most of the rest of the day. A foraging pig will find grass, grubs such as earthworms, roots and fallen fruit to supplement its diet in a healthy way. A confined pig needs to be 'busy' – perhaps searching out waste vegetables and roots as well as the balanced ration that you will be providing. Bagged pig feed is readily available and is designed for purpose; you can buy feeds that range from piglet creep feed to pet pig feeds. Pigs like wet feed and you can add surplus goat's milk to a feed in a trough.

A Fair Share

If you are raising more than one pig, then allow plenty of space, as shyer pigs will be pushed out and not get the feed they need. The other method is to throw the nuts over a wide area and leave the pigs to root for them, keeping them busy in the process.

Give Good Grass

If your pigs have access to good grass, they can consume up to 10 pounds or so a day, but the grass needs to be readily accessible. Seven pounds of good grass could replace about a pound of pig feed.

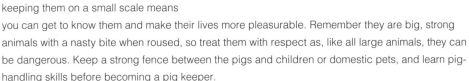

Handle With Care

Whatever the end objective for your pigs, keeping them on a small scale means you can get to know them and make their lives more pleasurable. Remember they are big, strong animals with a nasty bite when roused, so treat them with respect as, like all large animals, they can be dangerous. Keep a strong fence between the pigs and children or domestic pets, and learn pig-handling skills before becoming a pig keeper.

Everyday Care

Check your pigs first thing in the morning, give them clean water and food. Ensure they are not lame, that they are alert, interested

Top Tip

Feeding waste to pigs is strictly controlled, with any waste containing meat forbidden.

and, above all, keen on their food. Check their droppings are normal, not runny, and they have not been injured during the night. Check during the day and feed them again at night. If you shut them away for the night, then do so. Pigs require regular vaccinations and worming – your livestock vet will advise – and can also suffer from external parasites.

177

Three Acres and a Cow

As ruminants, cows require grass as a major part of their diet, so need a large area of grassland. When no fresh grass is available, they enjoy silage, haylage or hay to help their digestion. Concentrated cereal-based feed can form a small proportion of their diet, such as when forage (grass) provides insufficient energy or protein.

The Dairy Cow

The 'house cow' sounds such a cosy concept, but whether you have one cow or 10, remember you have taken on a huge commitment. The cow or cows must be milked every single day, usually at 12-hour intervals. Cows do have a 'dry' period, when they have no milk, at which time you could have a holiday, but otherwise you need to be there for them every day. So if you are the only person who milks, then you can never go more than a few hours away from the smallholding.

Her Needs

A cow's milk-production cycle is designed around the demands of her calf. It's quite low when the calf is born and increases to keep pace with the demands of the growing calf, for eight to 10 weeks, after which time, production will decrease, as the calf begins to utilize the grass. The milk will reduce considerably after nine or ten months, when she can stop producing and have a rest until the next calf arrives.

You really need more than one calf, as they need companionship. The cow will be distressed when she is separated from her new-born calf; be sure you can handle this. Gestation is nine months and she'll need to be put in calf again to obtain milk for the following year. This can be done by artificial insemination.

How Much Will She Eat?

Depending on the quality of the grass, she will need about one acre to graze all summer and a tonne of hay in winter. The calf will need extra feed and, if you have removed the calf early to get the milk, then you'll need to feed it milk several times a day by hand to start with, and then by a setup that, once the calf has learnt to drink, allows it to feed itself.

What You'll Need

There will be a lot of milk even from dual-purpose breeds, which will need processing and using. You'll have to set aside an area for a dairy and learn how to deal with milk. Whatever the breed, you'll need to be physically able to handle a large animal and have the necessary handling equipment. Also, the buildings must be laid out in a way that lets you safely and effectively handle the cows and they must be able to be washed down.

A cattle crush (or squeeze chute) is a useful piece of equipment for restraining cows for examining or veterinary treatment.

When milking, some facility for restraining the animals is required and vital for whenever veterinary treatment is necessary. It is strongly advised that you buy an experienced milker so that one of you knows what to do! Do not buy an unhandled cow and expect to be able to milk straight away.

Raising Cattle for Meat

If you have plenty of well-fenced pasture, raising for meat is the easier of the options for keeping cattle. There are several ways of doing this:

Buy Two-Year-Old Stores in the Spring

If you buy the right animals at the right price, then buying store cattle (*see* page 141) is the most straightforward way of raising cattle for meat. It's also a good way to gain some experience of cattle without committing yourself too deeply to begin with.

Each animal will require about 0.25 hectare (around half an acre) of good grazing and, if not sold in the autumn, will consume half a tonne of silage and 50 kg of concentrates each month during the winter.

You might consider for the first year getting a farmer to graze his cattle on your land in return for some meat and experience in cattle handling.

Buy Calves and Fatten Them

To be successful, you need to buy the right calves for fattening, not the cheapest calves – dairy breed calves are cheap but do not put on the weight. It is necessary to find a knowledgeable friend to go with you when purchasing calves, to guide and teach you how to select the good ones.

Rearing young calves is a skill, as nature intended them to be on their mother, and artificial

rearing is a poor substitute. The calf needs to be bright and healthy when you buy it and then you have to be spot on with the right quantities of milk, or feed milk-substitute regularly. The big danger with rearing calves is that they scour (have bad diarrhoea).

They will also need a warm, well-ventilated but draught-free building with lots of straw to keep the floor clean and dry.

Daily Care

This depends on which type of cattle you keep. Dairy cows require concentrated care and will consume large amounts of feed to produce their milk.

All cattle need to be checked at least twice a day – they should be alert, eating and not lame. The pasture also needs checking to see if there is sufficient food and that it is not becoming 'poached' – that is, muddy and with any grass trodden into the ground so it cannot drain.

Top Tip

Cattle, especially milking cows, need their feet trimming regularly, as any form of lameness stops them eating the large amount of food that they need.

182

Checklist

▶ **Less is more!** Do not overstock; understocking is much better, especially when you start.

▶ **Livestock are for life:** They require your time every morning, every evening and, at certain times of the year, even more time is needed.

▶ **Overestimate cost of equipment:** Setting up always costs more than you think it will.

▶ **The vet:** Your new best friend is your livestock vet. Register before you get livestock and don't hesitate to call them when you first start. Sick animals do not usually get better on their own.

▶ **Livestock is deadstock:** Even if your livestock is not destined for the table, do make plans for how you will cope with death. It is inevitable even with (or especially with) poultry.

▶ **Good facilities make for good husbandry:** Well-constructed, well-ventilated buildings make life better for owner and animals. Have as much hard standing (concrete, paving slabs) as you can and plenty of lighting. It is winter for a very long time!

▶ **Learning is never wasted:** Knowledge really is power, so learn as much as you can both theoretically and practically before you have livestock of your own.

▶ **Join the club:** The Breed Club and the smallholding club. Meeting like-minded people, many of whom have had years of experience, is a real shortcut to expertise.

Reaping Your Rewards

To Market, To Market

Producing from your smallholding is only part of the process. Selling is where you make your money. Luckily, today's smallholders have the power of the internet, which can be harnessed to help them make the most of their hard work.

Production Planning

Farmers worldwide have to plan their crops and livestock at least a year and usually more in advance. This is also true of smallholders. Imagine you produce, say, 15 turkeys for Christmas and you have done no advertising or pre-selling and you still have 15 turkeys after Christmas. You've borne all the costs and had no income, and still have to feed them.

Steps to Successful Selling

So you've grown your veg, picked your fruit, reared and 'finished' your animals, and now it's time to reap some hard-earned financial rewards. The amount of reward you can expect can be boosted by some strategic thinking before taking your wares to market:

▶ **Evaluate your market:** Will it be local, at a market or will you need to deliver further afield?

▶ **How will you let people know about your products?** This depends on your market, whether it is local, regional or countrywide.

▶ **How much can you spend on marketing?** Will it all be via social media such as Facebook, or do you need to print leaflets to give out at market? Do you need to advertise in a magazine or newspaper?

▶ **How will you present your products?** Looks count for a lot, so give careful consideration to your packaging. It can be very simple, but needs to be effective and eye-catching.

Is It Fit for Purpose?

Underpinning all the various regulations on marketing produce, there is one you must adhere to whether you are just selling to friends or at a market, and that is that whatever you sell must be 'fit for purpose'. It is your responsibility to ensure that the eggs are fresh and the fruit and veg are not rotten or worm-eaten.

At the Smallholding Gate

The simplest way of selling produce is at your gate or on your smallholding. This can range from a simple table with an 'honesty' box (where you trust people to put in the correct money) situated just outside your gate, or a farm shop that stocks products from other sources.

Beware the Law

Planning permission will normally be needed for most forms of sales at the smallholding, although seasonal selling on a portable stall will normally be overlooked. If you are selling surplus produce on an occasional basis, make sure you do not attract the planner's attention. For example, do not put out a stall on a dangerous road with no pull-in and where accidents could happen as a result.

Top Tip

Marketing begins before you sow the seed or hatch the egg.

At a Farmers' Market

Once, all markets were farmers' markets, where local growers took their livestock and produce to be sold into the local area. Then the convenience of supermarkets, supported by nationwide distribution systems, lured shoppers away. In recent times, however, there's been a resurgence of interest in farmers' markets, partly driven by people's desire to know just where their food has come from. Many countries now have hundreds or thousands of farmers' markets, which provide local food direct from the producers.

Insurance and Regulations

If you decide that farmers' markets are for you, then you will need some insurance. In the UK, for example, a minimum of £5 million Product Liability and Public Liability is recommended. You will also need to register with your local Environmental Health Officer (EHO) and follow any regulations relating to your particular foodstuffs. If selling any sort of cooked food such as jams, then find out the EHO's requirements and expect them to visit your premises.

Plan Costs and Choose Wisely

Although it seems a bit daunting, many small producers find farmers' markets an important source of income and also very sociable. You'll need to do your costs carefully regarding the

Top Tip

If you are selling eggs at your smallholding from a small flock (say under 20 hens), then this is quite legal as long as you don't grade them into sizes. If selling graded eggs or selling through someone else's shop or market, then they will need labelling.

cost of the stall, transport and even think about your time. The nearest farmers' market is not always the best one to go to. Do some homework and see which ones are busy.

Women's Institute Country Markets

The Women's Institute was formed in the UK in 1915 to revitalize rural communities and encourage women to become more involved in producing food during the First World War. Over a hundred years later, it is still at the forefront of home-baking and production, and their markets are well known. There are over 300 WI markets nationwide and they have the unique selling point of producing 'home-cooked' produce. Although you may still need to meet certain food hygiene regulations, this may be a more informal way to get into market trading, especially if your surplus is occasional.

Community Markets (Local Authority Run)

Many traditional town and village markets are struggling against the competition of supermarkets and out-of-town shopping centres. These are not farmers' markets, and often the goods come from far away, such as cheap clothes or end-of-line cosmetics. That said, the vegetable and food stalls can and do feature local food. Many of them are in need of support and the market manager will normally listen to good ideas and often offer reduced prices to new traders. Community markets are organized by the local authority or council, and stalls can be cheaper and more available than you might think, so it is well worth checking them out.

189

Selling Further Afield

The smallholding may be your world and occupy your every waking thought, but beyond your gate, there is a potentially global market waiting for your produce. There is a huge appetite from city dwellers for a more 'natural' way of living, so use the internet and tap into it.

Cast Your Net Wide

Some crops and produce may be suited to selling out of your immediate area. There are smallholders selling mutton, specialist breeds of lamb, bacon and rare-breed meat via the internet and offering delivery in specialist packaging. To do this requires a significant investment in meeting the regulations surrounding meat sales and transport, but such an enterprise can reap benefits in terms of greatly expanding your market. This is especially true if your native lambs live on the side of a remote hill and need to get to a city to realize their value.

Easier produce to sell by mail or delivery would be fleeces and their products, such as home-spun wool or dyed wool for felting, homemade garments or craft kits (do be sure to exploit the ever-growing crafting trend). It may also be possible to sell dried flowers or dry floral material in this way.

Using the Internet

There are so many online outlets that it is worth seeking out a marketing course that focuses on these virtual retailing opportunities and how to use them. As with any goods that are being sold, there are

Top Tip

It is less expensive selling online than through a physical store, but you will have to put in a lot of time to get visitors to your site and then keep them there through good service and delivery.

191

sale of goods regulations to protect the consumer and it is worth familiarizing yourself with these. One of the rules that is broken most often, mostly inadvertently, is weight, so pay close attention to this and there will be no risk of prosecution.

Top Tip

If the office manager doesn't like you selling your produce at work, you can confine your deliveries to the car park. But try to convince your workplace that this is a 'green' and progressive thing to be doing!

Success with Online Sales

▶ **Understand how social media works:** This will help you to get the best results. It's no good just posting once – it's an ongoing process.

▶ **Understand your market:** Internet users generally appreciate it when you get to the point quickly about what you are offering and why it is so good. Follow that by making it easy for them to purchase – use trusted methods of payment and offer PayPal.

▶ **The power of customer reviews:** If you let online buyers down with bad service or a poor product, they will go online to tell the world. Before you start trading, you need to ensure you can deliver what you say you can.

▶ **Harness social media:** Websites are needed as part of the process, but the online community has largely stopped browsing for websites and moved to social media. You must ensure that they are brought to your website by careful posts and use of social media.

▶ **Don't always sell when online:** An honest and amusing smallholding blog can bring people to your website and increase sales. As a smallholder, your unique selling point is you!

Keep It Simple, Stupid

Sometimes, the simplest and most effective ways of selling are ignored. If you or your family work outside the smallholding, then selling to your fellow employees is something to consider. Take a fresh basket of eggs into the office and watch them fly. (Remember to take egg boxes as well, but you should find that empty egg boxes will come back week on week to be refilled.) Okay, so you might get labelled as the mad egg lady, but who cares if you are shifting several dozen eggs a week?! You can do the same for all surplus produce.

Friends and Family

Don't feel you are being pushy if you tell them about what you have on offer; they will be pleased to buy fresh produce direct from a known source. But if you don't tell them, they can't buy. The same goes for any clubs or organizations that you belong to. Tell them what you have to sell.

Local Events

Local fêtes, table-top sales, ploughing days or even car boot sales can provide an outlet for surplus produce, are usually well advertised locally and low cost. They can be surprisingly effective for selling.

Preserving Your Harvest

To preserve the largesse of the summer so that people could eat through the winter was once a matter of life and death. Much of what we enjoy, such as bacon and ham, pickles and chutneys, jams and preserves, originated from the need to preserve. Bottling in alcohol is both delicious and a way of preserving fruit to eat in the winter. Today, we also have the option of freezing, and the old method of drying has been refined by use of specialist machinery.

Summer All Year Round

It's like a taste of summer when you take your homemade tomato and basil soup out of the freezer, open a jar of gooseberry jam or taste some bottled plums. Pickles and chutneys enhance the cold meat from the winter roasts.

All methods of preservation follow a basic method and once you have learnt a basic recipe for all of these methods, you can personalize it – adding herbs or spices to jam or using new combinations of fruit and vegetables for chutneys.

Pick Your Preserving Method

▶ **Jellies:** Clear preserves are notable for their deep, rich colours. The fruit pulp is strained out, leaving only the jelly. The deep colours of these make them very saleable.

▶ **Jams:** These include the crushed fruit and are a bit runnier than jellies.

▶ **Conserves:** Made with a mix of whole and crushed fruit, conserves contain more fruit than jam.

▶ **Pickles:** Can be vegetables or fruit, which are preserved using vinegar.

▶ **Chutneys**: A mix between jams and pickles, with very varied flavours, but normally sweet and sour. There's huge scope for creativity in making these – you can put almost anything into a chutney – but the best ones manage to keep at least some of the ingredients quite firm and identifiable.

▶ **Relishes:** More highly spiced pickles or chutneys.

▶ **Marmalades:** Like jams but made only from citrus fruits and often including shreds of the peel. They can also be a pure jelly.

▶ **Mincemeat:** More scope for creativity, but usually includes minced dried fruits, grated or cooked apples, and flavoured with spices and sometimes alcohol. (It was developed to preserve minced meat although this is rarely used today.)

▶ **Bottling:** Uses syrup and heat to preserve and, of all the methods, must be done correctly for it to be safe.

▶ **Salting:** A very old method sometimes used today for runner beans. It will taste quite salty when used.

▶ **Freezing:** Ideal for most forms of produce, though some are better 'blanched' (dipped in boiling water first). Soft fruit can be flattened and frozen on baking trays. It won't be as it was when you unfreeze it, but it will be fine for making jams and puddings, and this is a really helpful option when you have a glut of soft fruit.

A Few Basic Rules

Before you start on the road to preservation, there are a few rules that, if observed, will make life easier and ensure perfect results every time:

▶ Be aware of pectin content: Pectin is essential to get jam to set. It's important to know which fruits contain pectin naturally and which need it added. Strawberries, blackberries and cherries are all low in pectin. Additional pectin is found in jam sugar, can be bought as pectin or you can add apples or gooseberries, which contain it naturally. Or, the acidity of lemon juice can help jell the pectin.

▶ **Ensure that all the ingredients are in perfect condition:** If you have either under- or overripe fruit that you wish to use, it is better to mix the two together. That way, the underripe fruit will give a good amount of pectin, while the overripe fruit has the colour and flavour. But it is a juggling act to get the correct balance. Do not use rotten or badly damaged fruit or vegetables or those that look as though they are going bad, as this may taint the finished taste.

▶ **Prepare your produce:** Wash it thoroughly or peel thinly, discarding the skin and pips if required by the recipe. Cut the fruit or vegetables into equal-size pieces. Remember, in marmalade, the skin and pips are used, but not the bitter white pith, which is discarded.

▶ **Prepare your work area:** Ensure you have all the ingredients and tools before starting.

▶ **Do not use copper, brass or iron pots and utensils:** The acid in the fruit will react with the metal and spoil the finished result.

▶ **Never turn your back on it:** Make sure it does not burn; otherwise you will have to discard it.

▶ **Jam gets very hot:** Be careful when handling the hot, sticky liquid and keep children and animals away from the kitchen.

197

Getting Jammy

Making jam is such a cost-effective way to use soft fruit and when the skill is mastered, might even be a source of income in the sale of jams and jellies.

Blackberry & Apple Jam

Fills about 8 x 450 g/1 lb jars

1.8 kg/4 lb ripe blackberries
300 ml/½ pint water
700 g/1½ lb cooking apples (peeled weight)
2.75 kg/6 lb preserving sugar

Remove and discard any remaining hulls from the blackberries and wash well. Place in a heavy-based saucepan and add half the water. Place over a gentle heat and bring to the boil. Simmer gently, stirring occasionally, for 10–15 minutes until the blackberries are soft. Remove and reserve while cooking the apples.

Peel the apples, discarding the core, and then chop. Place in a preserving pan with the remaining water and place over a gentle heat. Simmer for 12–15 minutes, stirring occasionally with a wooden spoon, until the apples are soft and pulpy. Mash with a spoon or potato masher until a pulp is formed with no large lumps.

Add the blackberries to the apple pulp, then stir in the sugar. Place over a gentle heat and cook for 10 minutes, or until the sugar has dissolved. Bring to the boil and boil rapidly until setting point is reached (when the jam reaches 105°C/220°F when tested off the boil). Allow to cool for at least 5 minutes before potting and labelling.

198

Jellies

Jellies are made in a similar way to jams, but are strained so they are clear and usually deep in colour. They must set.

Fresh Mint Jelly

Fills about 6 x 225 g/8 oz jars

2.25 kg/5 lb Bramley cooking apples
1.25 litres/2¼ pints water
bunch fresh mint, plus 2 tbsp freshly chopped mint
1.5 litres/2½ pints vinegar
allow 450 g/1 lb preserving sugar per 600 ml/1 pint liquid
green food colouring (optional)

Wash the apples and chop (do not peel or core), add to the preserving pan with the water and mint. Bring to the boil; simmer for 1 hour. Add the vinegar and boil for 5 minutes.

Top Tip

The easiest way to test for a set is with a jam/sugar thermometer.

Cool slightly before straining through a jelly bag. Once all the juice has been extracted, measure and pour into the preserving pan. Add the sugar. Place over a gentle heat and cook, stirring frequently, until the sugar has completely dissolved.

Add a few drops of green food colouring, if using. Bring to the boil and boil rapidly for 10–15 minutes until setting point is reached (*see* opposite and tip above). Remove and cool for at least 5 minutes. Skim if necessary, then stir in the chopped mint. Pot, cover and label.

199

Fruit Cheeses and Butters

These are both variations on the jam method. Often eaten with cold meat, they are particularly welcome in the winter.

Thick Damson Cheese

Fills about 4 x 350 g/12 oz jars

1.8 kg/4 lb ripe damsons
300 ml/½ pint water
150 ml/¼ pint freshly squeezed
  orange juice
2 tbsp finely grated orange zest
allow 350 g/12 oz granulated sugar to each 600 ml/1 pint pulp

Wash the damsons and cut in half and discard the stones and any of the damsons that are damaged or bad. Place in a nonreactive saucepan or preserving pan. Add the water with the orange juice and finely grated orange zest. Cook for 12–15 minutes, stirring occasionally, until the damsons have completely collapsed.

Sieve, then measure, the damson pulp and return to the rinsed pan. Stir in the sugar and heat, stirring constantly, until the sugar has completely dissolved. Continue to cook for a further 15–20 minutes until a thick, creamy consistency is achieved. Pot into warm sterilized jars, cover and label.

200

Spiced Apple Butter

Fills about 3 x 350 g/12 oz jars

1.5 kg/3 lb cooking apples
1.1 litres/2 pints apple juice
300 ml/½ pint water and lemon juice
  mixed together
3 –4 star anise
4–6 green cardamom pods
pared zest of 1 lemon
allow 350 g/12 oz granulated sugar
  for each 600 ml/1 pint pulp

Wash and chop the apples (do not peel or core), discarding any damaged pieces. Place in a preserving pan together with the apple juice and water.

Wrap the spices and zest in a piece of muslin tied with a long piece of string. Place in the pan and tie the string to the pan handle.

Bring to the boil, then simmer gently for 30 minutes, stirring occasionally, or until the apples have completely collapsed. Discard the muslin bag.

Sieve, then measure, the apple pulp and return to the rinsed pan. Stir in the sugar and heat, stirring constantly, until the sugar has completely dissolved. Continue to cook for a further 15–20 minutes until a thick, creamy consistency is achieved. Pot into warm sterilized jars, cover and label.

201

Choose Chutney

Chutneys are easy and you can be endlessly creative with your combinations. Allow your creativity free rein once you have mastered the basic principles. Unlike jam, you can use less than perfect ingredients such as unripe tomatoes, overgrown veg such as marrows or pumpkins, blemished apples and pears and even woody roots – after processing, they will taste delicious. It's simpler than jam making, as you don't have to worry about pectin and setting point.

Everyday Spiced Vinegar

This is an essential ingredient for making chutneys.

Makes 750 ml/1¼ pints

6 tsp peppercorns

3 tsp mustard seeds

2 tsp allspice

1 blade mace

1 large cinnamon stick, bruised

4 fresh bay leaves

1 small piece root ginger, chopped

1 tbsp salt

750 ml/1¼ pints malt vinegar

Tie all the spices into a piece of muslin and place in a nonreactive saucepan. Add 225 ml/8 fl oz of the vinegar and bring to the boil. Add the remaining vinegar and boil for a further 3 minutes.

Remove from the heat and leave covered for at least 24 hours. Strain into sterilized bottles and screw the caps on tightly.

Marrow Chutney

Fills about 5 x 450 g/ 1 lb jars

1 large marrow, about 1.8 kg/ 4 lb in weight

1–2 tbsp salt

300 g/11 oz onion (about 2 onions)

3 garlic cloves

450 g/12 oz cooking apples

50 g/2 oz fresh root ginger, grated

1 tsp ground cinnamon

1 tsp ground cloves

225 g/8 oz light muscovado sugar

900 ml/1½ pints spiced vinegar (see opposite)

225 g/8 oz dried fruit, such as dates, finely chopped

Cut the marrow in half and discard the seeds and peel. Cut into small chunks. Layer in a colander, sprinkling each layer with salt. Leave for 30 minutes, then rinse the chunks and place in a preserving pan.

Peel and chop the onions, garlic and apples and add to the marrow together with the spices, sugar and vinegar. Place over a gentle heat and bring to the boil. Reduce the heat to a simmer and cook for 25 minutes, stirring occasionally.

Add the dried fruit and simmer for a further 20 minutes until the vinegar is absorbed and a thick consistency is reached.

When cooked, remove from the heat and cool for 5 minutes. Stir and pot in warm sterilized jars, cover and label.

Top Tip

Other squash can be used in this recipe, such as butternut or acorn.

203

Pickled in Vinegar

Pickles are not to be confused with chutneys, as these preserve whole or sliced veg in a spicy vinegar. The biggest difficulty with pickles is keeping the veg (such as cucumbers) crisp.

Pickled Red Cabbage

Fills about 4 x 450 g/1 lb jars

1 red cabbage, 1.25 kg/2½ lb in weight
1.5 litres/2½ pints vinegar
salt

Choose firm cabbages that feel heavy and are a good colour. Cut off a slice about 1 cm/½ inch thick from the stalk end and discard. Remove the outside leaves and cut the cabbage into quarters. Discard the central core from each quarter. Using a very sharp knife, shred the cabbage as thinly as possible.

Using a large glass mixing bowl, arrange a layer of the shredded cabbage in the base about 2.5 cm/1 inch high. Sprinkle with a layer of salt, then cover with a further layer of cabbage and then salt. Repeat the layering until all the cabbage has been used, finishing with a layer of salt. Cover and leave overnight in a cool place.

Next day, drain, then rinse the cabbage thoroughly and shake off any excess water. Pack into sterilized jars to within 2.5 cm/1 inch of the top of each jar. Pour in sufficient spiced vinegar to cover the cabbage. Cover with nonmetallic lids.

Using and Preserving Herbs

Herbs can be frozen flat in plastic bags or in ice cubes to be used for flavouring during the winter.

Herb Salt

These are a lot cheaper to make than to buy. You'll need to dry your fresh herbs for this so they don't dampen the salt. Simply combine 225 g of salt (approximately 8 oz) with whichever herbs you fancy. Why not try using dried parsley and chives, for example? Store in an airtight jar and use to flavour salad dressings or casseroles.

Herb Sugar

This is a similar idea to herb salt, with lavender being a real favourite. Bruise the leaves of the fresh herbs; don't make them mushy. You'll need a couple of sprigs per 450 g (1 lb) sugar. Add the sugar to the bruised herbs, stirring gently. Place in airtight jars for a couple of days in a cool place. Stir again to stop the sugar clumping and to distribute the herb essence. It will take about two weeks of stirring every other day or so. Ideal for flavouring puddings, ice cream and for dusting cakes and fresh fruit salad.

Herb Bags

These are also known as bouquet garni. Cut squares of butter muslin or similar and combine ½ teaspoon of thyme to ¼ teaspoon basil and marjoram plus a bay leaf. You can also add peppercorns. Make a stock of these and they can be added to soups, stews and casseroles. You can vary the ingredients according to your tastes. As well as items for sale, these make superb presents for friends.

Salting

A method not often used today, but many smallholders still like to keep the old traditions alive, so here is how to make salted runner beans:

You need roughly a kilo (2¼ lb) of salt to 4 kg (8¾ lb) of beans, but in reality, you probably won't measure it. You must use a glass bottle or a stone crock, and you put a layer of salt, then a layer of sliced beans, then a layer of salt and so on, until you reach the top of the container. Seal tightly and store in a cool place. Use as needed, but remember to wash well before cooking.

Storing Eggs

Eggs keep for a very long time in a cool place or in the fridge. They can keep for anything from five to nine weeks (although it's advisable to check them towards the end of that period). If an egg is bad, it lets you know by a truly revolting smell, so there can be no doubt.

Top Tip

You can store eggs in the freezer for use in cooking, out of their shells and usually in beaten egg form.

The shells are porous, so will absorb any strong smells of food nearby. Before eggs were available all year round, people preserved them in water glass (sodium silicate). Water glass seals the pores of eggs, meaning they keep much longer.

Home Cider Making

The process of making cider at home is relatively straightforward, although there are a few pitfalls to be aware of. Once you've mastered the technique, you'll have the satisfaction of home-grown hangovers! (Drink responsibly.)

Any Apple Will Do

Cider can be made from almost any type of apple, with ripe windfalls being ideal. (There are specific cider-making varieties if you want to get serious about it.) If you can mix some dessert and cooking apples, that will give a dryer taste, and a few crab apples will give it even more dryness. If you only have one variety or you don't know what they are, don't worry, as they will make a perfectly respectable cider. The fruit does need to be ripe, not only so the juice can be extracted, but also because their sugar level will be high and that's what will make the alcohol.

But Do Reject These...

You should take out apples that are already fermenting or rotten and those with occupants such as maggots. Watch out for wasps as you collect the apples.

First Press the Apples

Small crushers make this job much easier and many farms and villages have apple days, when you can take your apples to be crushed and pressed. Other methods include

207

crushing in a bucket, putting in a mangle and even mincing, but if you are going to do this every year, you will want to invest in a small press. You can feed the leftover waste pulp to pigs, or in smaller quantities to other animals, but don't let it ferment – it will be quick to do this. Your compost heap is also a good recipient.

Simple Steps to Cider

▶ **Yeast or sugar (optional):** Cider makers differ in how they make cider, with some adding cultured yeast. But traditional cider was made using only apples, as they contain enough natural yeast to ferment. Sugar can be added to increase the strength of the cider (about half a kilo to five litres).

▶ **Ferment your juice:** The time it takes to ferment depends on the apples, the temperature outside and the sugar level, but it can take anything from a few weeks to a few months. The liquid will stop bubbling, start to clear and taste clean and not too sweet. If you prefer not to guess, you can use a hydrometer.

▶ **Let it settle:** The cider is then 'racked off' into jugs or bottles in a cool place and left to settle. There may be some secondary fermentation, so don't fill to the top of the bottles. Again, there are variations on this method, with some makers racking off after the first fermentation and leaving to ferment in barrels or containers, and others racking off twice and adding sugar at racking off.

▶ **Record your progress:** Even superb cider makers have disasters, and one major cider producer converts the liquid to cider vinegar if it goes wrong! Always write down each stage of the process so you can try to work out what the problem was and avoid repeating it.

You can use a hydrometer to measure the 'specific gravity' (relative density) of your cider – if it measures 1.000 or below the fermentation is finished.

208

Checklist

▶ **Is it good and safe?** As a basic, all food sold must be 'fit for purpose'. Use clean equipment for all preserves and never reuse lids. Store all produce in a cool, dry place where vermin cannot contaminate it.

▶ **Keep records:** Do this even if selling on a small scale, so if someone complains about your eggs, you can be sure of the exact day you collected them.

▶ **Be sure you want to sell meat:** Meat has a lot of regulations surrounding it; to produce it on a commercial scale, you will need to make a considerable investment in equipment and buildings.

▶ **Get the word out:** Use the internet for your marketing and learn how to get the best from social media.

▶ **Kitchen check:** For kitchen-made products such as jams, you will have to have your kitchen checked by the authorities. Many people do this quite satisfactorily, so don't let it put you off.

▶ **Sell-by dates:** If selling jams and preserves or even honey, you'll need to know the date it was made and have a sell-by date on the label. Labelling regulations do change, so keep up to date.

▶ **Don't grade eggs:** Eggs produced on your smallholding can be sold on your smallholding without labelling if you do not grade them.

▶ **Experiment:** Master the basic jam, jelly, pickling and chutney recipes and you can experiment and make your own flavours.

Pests
and
Problems

Learning From Experience

'Help, this is not what I thought would happen on my smallholding! No one warned me about this and now I don't know what to do!' Smallholding can be an amazing experience, but it takes a lot of effort. This book is here to help you in those first stages and to tell you not to worry, most things can be fixed and all experiences are positive and will help you to learn. Here are some of the commonest problems that happen in the first few years of smallholding.

Planning Problems

'My local council is saying that I need planning permission for my smallholding enterprise. This is going to cost me money and there is no guarantee that I will succeed.'

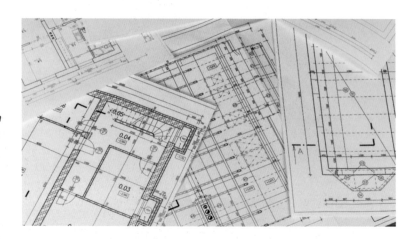

Check Before You Buy

Not getting the appropriate planning permissions for what you want to do on your smallholding is one of the major reasons for things going very wrong. As mentioned at the beginning of this book, before you even buy a property, you need to be sure that you can do the things you want to do on it and that all

Top Tip

Be realistic about your chances of getting planning permission.

planning permissions you need are in place. It is often assumed that agricultural properties have free rein to erect buildings and barns, but they don't, especially if they are on small acreages of land and are in a national park. There are also changes of use that sometimes need to be sorted – they don't always apply, but it is worth checking. For example, if you are going from agricultural to equine, some planning authorities will require a change of use.

Consider Your Longer-Term Plans

If your chosen property has neighbours and you decide to take up pig keeping or rear cockerels, you could also fall foul of environmental laws. If something you do is deemed a nuisance to others around you, then you may encounter problems. It's worth considering before you buy.

Will You Want to Build?

If you are looking to build a house in open countryside, then you may well be unsuccessful. There is a rural myth that if you keep animals, then you are automatically given planning permission so you can care for them. Not true. To get planning permission out of the building area and in open countryside is a challenge, and you will have to put up a very good case as to why you should be given it. It will require reports of environmental impact, detailed business studies and the hiring of experts to make your case and you still may not be successful. If you buy land without planning permission for a house, then you cannot assume that one day you will get the permission. It is a huge gamble.

How to Get Planning Permission

Seek a meeting with the planners to find out exactly what it is they want. It may be a mere formality and very straightforward to achieve, or it might be more complex but still possible. There is a cost of applying for planning permission and on top of that, you may need to pay for drawings of proposed buildings. You might be seeking planning permission for a change of use to something more commercial; even a small home business such as jam making might require this. The planners are looking to see how much it will change the character of the area and will be asking questions such as how it will change the volume of traffic.

Planning Pointers

The following preparatory steps will help you navigate the typical planning system:

▶ **Meeting:** Seek an informal pre-planning meeting with your local planning department.

▶ **Look at the local plan for the area:** This can show you areas for future development and conservation areas.

▶ **Check out the community-led plan:** If one exists – such as a 'parish plan' (a plan of actions and aspirations of a community) available from your parish or local authority –familiarize yourself with this too.

Top Tip

Know your local authorities. Parish councils are advisory and their views on your planning will be forwarded to the local council, either the district if you have one or to the county council. It is the local council that has the final say, not the parish council, though it is good to get them on side.

▶ **How will you affect others?** Critically assess if your plans will impinge on anyone near you or affect traffic flow.

▶ **Business plan:** Ensure you have a realistic and achievable business plan.

▶ **Take it step by step:** Don't be put off if you really want to do something. There is impartial and free advice available from such bodies as the Citizens Advice Bureau and Planning Aid.

▶ **Make sure you understand how the system works:** Check out relevant sites such as England's Planning Aid website: www.rtpi.org.uk/planning-aid.

Veterinary Fees

'My vet's bill is huge!'

When you begin to keep livestock, you are not sure what constitutes a life-threatening experience and what you can deal with yourself. Initially, you will have to consult the vet more often than you will need to further on in your smallholding career.

Consider It an Investment

Consider vet's bills an investment in the future, as you will learn from each visit and develop a relationship with your vet. Your vet's bills will decrease with experience, but in the meantime, budget for veterinary support as a learning cost. Above all, your livestock must not suffer.

Educate Yourself

Attending courses will really help, especially with lambing. These use a box to contain a simulation of a ewe's uterus and birth canal and you deliver long-dead lambs through the actual bones of a ewe's pelvis. This will give you real confidence in knowing when, and more importantly when not, to intervene in lambing. If you intend to lamb, offer to help with lambing before you undertake this yourself. The value of experience cannot be overestimated.

Most livestock vets have livestock evenings, so make the effort to attend them. You can also get a wealth of information from online sources, for example:

▶ **The National Animal Disease Information Service:** NADIS publishes a monthly Parasite Forecast for farmers and livestock keepers, based on detailed Met Office data: www.nadis.org.uk.

▶ **The Sustainable Control of Parasites:** SCOPs gives information on worming and also provides parasite forecasts: www.scops.org.uk.

Top Tip

When starting out, don't hesitate to call the vet; most health situations don't resolve themselves and only get worse.

Overstocking

'I've lambed this year and it all went well and now I have twice the number of sheep. Should I feed more hay as the grass is very short and some of the paddock is rather muddy?'

Top Tip

It can't be repeated enough: with all livestock, understock rather than overstock.

In the short term, yes, feed hay and concentrates (sheep nuts) and provide a good mineral lick. In the longer term, reduce the number of livestock on the acreage. Overgrazed grass is not going to improve, so no paddock should have to support more sheep that it is able to.

Sell or Find New Pasture

If you are really sure that you don't want to sell some of the sheep, then you must find other grazing so that the grass on your paddock can rest and regain its vigour. You cannot go on overstocking and over-grazing year after year without significant damage to your grassland, with a possible increased worm burden for your sheep and the need to feed expensive bought-in feeds to maintain your flock's health. Grass is the best feed for growing sheep and you must ensure that your flock has plenty available.

Problems With Poultry

'My laying flock of poultry is supposed to lay around 270–300 eggs a year per bird, but they have stopped laying. How do I get them to start again?'

Are They in Moult?

All hens have to go into a moult, so it could be that they are in that process. If so, then they need to be given nutritionally well-balanced feed, so don't cut their normal food just because they are not laying.

Is Their Feed Adequately Nutritious?

If they are not in moult, then you need to evaluate what you are feeding. Modern hybrids cannot live on kitchen scraps and wheat; they need a well-balanced diet in the form of laying pellets in the morning,

with a scratch feed of wheat and other corn in the afternoon. In the short term, supply a vitamin and mineral supplement in their water and, if not feeding laying pellets, then introduce them. You may need a higher level of protein in your layers' pellets than those you are currently using. Consult with your agricultural merchant.

Could They Have Worms?

If feeding is not the problem, then consider whether they might be carrying a worm burden. There are some excellent wormers on the market,

219

including Flubenvet, which can also be purchased as part of a feed ration. It is very effective. If using a herbal-type wormer (or indeed any wormer), be sure to get the faeces analysed to check that the poultry are free of worms.

Could They Have Mites?

Another reason for a drop in laying is an infestation of red mite. These suck the blood out of the bird and can cause death, but firstly they will cause a drop in laying.

Hybrids need a well-balanced diet that includes laying pellets.

Always treat poultry houses and runs for red mite and consider treating the birds too. You will feel the red mite on you if you handle the birds. Treat red mite as a life-threatening situation and have a plan for routine treatment.

Are They Getting Enough Food and Water?

Another possibility is that the flock of hens is not receiving sufficient food and water, and this could be due to not having enough feeders and drinkers. Shy hens will not feed with those higher up the pecking order, so always supply sufficient numbers of feeders and drinkers so that all the flock get enough food and water.

220

Problems With Predators

'Yesterday evening, something killed most of my chickens and ducks. How can I prevent this happening?'

Poultry especially are at risk from many predators who want to do them harm or eat them. It is your responsibility to keep your stock safe from these predators, which come in many forms: winged, four-legged and even sometimes two-legged.

Poultry Enemy Number One: The Fox

Foxes are perhaps top of the poultry keeper's list when it comes to predators. In theory, they are nocturnal hunters, so if you shut your poultry in at dusk, they should be safe. In practice, foxes can and do hunt in the daytime and in towns and cities, they seem to be awake all day long. Also, when the time of the year during which the female has growing cubs coincides with short, dark nights, hunger – the need for her to feed her family as well as herself – means they come out in the day for more chances of food.

▶ **Keep them out:** The best method for most poultry keepers is prevention, which is to keep poultry confined in fox-proof houses and strongly fenced runs except when there is someone outside with them, such as weekends spent in the garden. Always make sure that the poultry are shut up when they go in to roost at dusk, even if that means asking neighbours.

▶ **Can you get rid of foxes?** There are many obvious barriers – legal, moral, social and practical – to lethally disposing of foxes. Successful disposal is a job for an expert marksman, and trapping still involves killing the animal, which must be done humanely. In any case, any attempts to eradicate a fox from the area are likely to be in vain – foxes are territorial, so as soon as you get rid of one, another one will move in.

► **Deterrence:** The presence of dogs can help to deter foxes, though you will need to train your own dog well not to touch or chase the birds, and you must be wary of other people's. Also, it is well worth trying some of the chemical and ultrasonic repellents that are on the market.

The Weasel Family

Weasels and stoats are small, so can squeeze through any tiny gaps into the house, where they will wreak havoc and cause deaths. Be sure that the house is secure, and check regularly. Mink can be a problem in some areas. They usually kill at night, so make sure the poultry are securely shut away. Mink normally only live near water.

Other Four-legged Predators

These include raccoons (in the USA), polecats (and escaped ferrets), bobcats and badgers who are looking for eggs. As with all the others, protect your poultry with secure housing, meticulous attention to shutting them in at night and well-constructed runs.

Winged Predators

Winged predators, in the form of certain types of hawk, owls, crows, jays and magpies, are capable of harming birds and young chickens; chicks and small bantams are particularly at risk. Most varieties of raptor are protected and cannot be killed, so protect your poultry. If you have a big problem with this, you may have to net the run.

Problems With Pests

'My smallholding is overrun with rats and mice. They are eating my wild bird food. I think they might even be in the house!'

The Laws of Rodent Control

▶ **The first law** of rodent control is to take action when you see even one rat. Rats have a large territory, and if you see one, there will be plenty of others nearby.

▶ **The second law** is that any pest control must only target that creature and not be a danger to other creatures, such as your domestic pets and wildlife, for example owls, who might eat rats.

▶ **The third law** is that it must be as humane as possible. Just because it is a pest to you does not mean that it cannot feel pain.

Target Their Food Source

Rats (and mice) only populate smallholdings for one reason and that reason is to feed. So prevention centres on them not being able to easily get food. It is often said that poultry attract rats and mice, but it is not the poultry, it is the food and warm breeding conditions.

▶ **Feeders:** It is very hard not to have any surplus food around the smallholding, and most people will fill up poultry feeders in the morning and leave for the poultry to use all day. There are some

Chicken-operated auto feeder.

223

excellent automatic feeders on the market, which the
poultry operate themselves or which dispense food at
regular intervals. These greatly cut down the availability
of food (and will also discourage wild birds).

Top Tip

Prevention is always better than control.

▶ **Storage:** Feed storage is important. A metal container that cannot
be gnawed is ideal. In a major rodent infestation, even plastic
will get chewed through. If you have limited storage, do not order
more food than you can store.

▶ **Manure and compost heaps:** These are warm places containing
food and are often populated by rats. Situate them away from the
smallholding and from other food sources.

Ways To Eradicate Rats and Mice

▶ **Shooting:** This is the most humane, as it does not involve poison. You will need to be a good shot, as
injuring is not acceptable. Get the rats to come to a place to feed and sit quietly and wait for them.
You can easily find people who are experienced in shooting and will come for a small fee.

▶ **Poisoning:** This is a commonly used method. There is a correct and safe way to do this – randomly
putting poison round your smallholding is not acceptable. Pest control companies will bait where
other animals and birds cannot reach the poison. The bait container must be tamper-proof. Most
rats will return to their nests after eating the poison and die there, but you need to consult with an
expert on how to lay the bait to avoid rats being caught by cats or dogs, or poisoning wildlife.

▶ **Rat traps:** There are two types of rat traps: those that kill as the rat enters them and those that

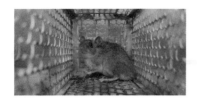

capture the rat alive. If you choose a live trap, you must check twice daily and be prepared to shoot the rat. Under no circumstances drown the rat, as this is not humane.

▶ **Dogs:** Some breeds of dog, such as Jack Russell terriers, are proficient at catching and killing rats. Ensure that the dog's vaccinations are all up to date and that it receives regular worming and flea treatment. Always be aware that a rat bite could be very dangerous to the dog and seek immediate veterinary treatment should that occur.

▶ **Cats:** Not all cats are good at rat catching. Imagine wrestling a Doberman-type dog and you can see the challenge that the average cat has with killing an animal the size of a rat. But keeping cats on your smallholding will have a big effect on the mouse population and act as a deterrent to cats, plus they will often tackle the youngs rats. All cats should be neutered, and given a warm, dry place to sleep and fresh water. They must be fed on a daily basis and not expected to rely on mice and rats for food. Cats have a strong hunting instinct and will hunt and kill without being hungry. Your local cat sanctuary often will have feral cats needing yard homes and will help you to settle them in. As with dogs, the cats should be vaccinated and wormed.

225

Problems Settling In

'We've moved to the country and my teenagers hate it. My husband is hardly ever at home in the week as he is working and I am left to do all the work.'

This is why the careful questions you ask yourself and your family before you move are so important. Be really honest about the time left over from working and never underestimate the stress of commuting a long way to get to work, or the effect that living in a remote rural location will have on the family. Children usually adore the countryside, while teenagers are often frustrated by not being able to see their friends or access entertainment.

Help Along Their Social Life

Planning will help to overcome this, as will getting to know local parents of teenagers so that your children can have a social life. There are even 'young farmers' organizations that stage gatherings and events. Make sure you factor in driving lessons and a car.

Don't Take on Too Much

If you are left on your own all week, don't undertake more than you can comfortably do on your own. Finally, don't be frightened to scale back a bit if you have to; you can realize your dreams later on when circumstances change.

226

Checklist

▶ **Failure to plan is planning to fail:** Think through the full consequences of every decision.

▶ **Seek professional advice early on:** Whether it is a veterinary problem, a planning issue, a rodent problem or something else altogether, don't let small problems become really big ones by not taking any action.

▶ **Seek the wisdom around you:** Use your fellow smallholders via your smallholding club to see what their solutions are to problems – your experiences are not unique.

▶ **Go online:** Use all the wonderful information on the internet to check out solutions to problems and prevention action. There are many professional websites offering advice completely free of charge.

▶ **Take it easy:** Enjoy your smallholding and don't feel you have to do things if you are finding them hard or not enjoying them. Make your smallholding work for you as well as the other way round!

Taking Things Further

Adding to Your Acreage

When thinking of increasing your land, you might want to consider the option of renting rather than buying. Obviously, this decision comes down to how much money you have available, or whether you can borrow more to fund your new land. It also depends on whether you can actually find something suitable within your area.

Buying Land

Most areas have a rough guide of the price for agricultural land in their area. However, this does not mean that the three acres down the road will be that price. The seller will get whatever they can for the land, and if it is a pony paddock, then you can reckon on the cost being far more than agricultural land. If the land is next to your house, the owner will calculate the value that it is to you and adjust the price accordingly. You will need to negotiate with the seller, but ultimately they fix the price.

Funding Your Purchase

Banks will often look favourably at land and allow you to

increase your mortgage. They may want proof that it
is worth what you paid for it. Alternatively, if you are
buying it to increase an enterprise or start another,
they will need a business plan of how you will get a
return from the land.

Top Tip

Don't forget to factor in the cost of what will
go on the land as well as the land itself!

Extra Factors

Any land has to have a safe boundary. Be sure to factor in the cost of fencing. The land also needs
to have water, or you will have to make arrangements to provide it on a daily basis. This will limit the
number of animals you keep, as all livestock drink a surprisingly large amount of water and it's difficult
to transport the stuff. Look at the quality of the grazing or, if you are planning to grow field crops, the soil
type. Does it flood? Has it been overgrazed? What weeds are prevalent? Are there any poisonous plants
that must be removed?

Renting Land

It can be hard to find anything within a built-up village area, as 'in-fill' planning has meant that
most open spaces have been built on. But you might find some short-term grazing that is awaiting
building. Going out of the village or away from your holding lends extra importance to finding
somewhere safe for your livestock – so not on a main road, if possible. The fencing will be erected
either by the landlord or, more usually, by yourself. Be clear whose responsibility this is. It is likely
you will have to maintain it.

Tenant Farms

For most, it is not affordable to buy even a small farm, though there are some areas of the UK, such as
some parts of Scotland and Wales, where prices are competitive. In the UK, there is an option to rent on an

Agricultural Tenancy, and tenant farms are a long-established system around the world. Most rented farms will require some evidence that you have the experience and skills to keep the land in good order.

In a few counties around the UK, there are still County Council Farms that offer a good assured length of renting. Cambridgeshire's Farms Estate, for example, comprises 13,400 hectares and has 197 farm tenants. In England and Wales, there are over 3,100 tenants on 111,000 hectares of local authority land. The Cambridgeshire estate is the largest. Again, you will need to be able to prove that you can manage the farm and give your plans as to what you are going to do.

How Much Should You Expect to Pay?

Rent depends on the area in which you live, the size of the field and the type of land. The landlord can really set whatever price they want and you need to decide if the land is worth it to you. There should be a contract with notice required by both parties, especially if you have had to invest money putting up stock-proof fencing. Also use the contract to agree any individual requirements. With ponies and horses, there may be restrictions on grazing; they may want them removed for certain times of the year to rest the grazing, or it is often part of an agreement that the droppings are regularly picked up. For other livestock, there may be a stocking rate that you mustn't exceed (though never overstock, because it causes health problems).

Dos and Don'ts of Renting

Happy renting means understanding and agreeing the terms and conditions on both sides and paying your rent regularly. Make sure there are no hidden extras, such as water rates. Always keep the land in good order, not only for the sake of your animals or crops, but also out of respect to the owner. Do not erect buildings without permission – in many areas, planning permission from the local council is also needed.

Adding Value to Your Smallholding

This could be adding value to the crops or items that you are already producing, utilizing your smallholding for other uses, or using it as a base for business.

Whether it is making cheese from your goats' milk, offering up your land for caravan storage, providing access to your smallholding for tourism, courses or care farming (the therapeutic use of farming-related activities), doing up classic cars and vehicles or running a gardening business, all of these are going to require some business expertise and a good marketing strategy, and most will require some investment.

Deciding How to Take Things Further

Having now experienced practical life on your smallholding, you can ask and answer the following questions more accurately:

▶ What am I **naturally good at**?

▶ What does my smallholding **lend itself to**?

▶ How much **surplus income** can I spare to develop my new enterprise?

▶ Will my **family** be able to help me with my enterprise?

▶ What **skills** do I have and what do I need?

▶ What **time** do I have to devote to it?

What Am I Good At?

Be honest. This may not be the thing you thought you wanted to do when you started. Also consider what you really detest doing and don't feel you do all that well. If you are going to invest time and money in something, you need to be totally committed to it.

Case Study

Sally Ann came into smallholding enthusiastically to be more or less self-sufficient. She reared pigs and sheep and kept poultry. But although she quite enjoyed parts of it, her heart was still with her first love, horses. Finally, she made the decision to cut right down on the livestock to just a few for her own freezer and to free up the space to have some full liveries, where she did all the work and charged accordingly. She decided to invest in a manège. Her smallholding had access to country riding for her clients.

What Does My Smallholding Lend Itself To?

When you first move, it's often hard to judge your smallholding's strengths and weaknesses. Sometimes it is something you didn't even consider: it is on the tourism trail or next to a right of way, which you thought would be a nuisance but from which you are now making money by selling eggs to passers-by. Maybe you find out something about the locality that you can use to your advantage, such as a nearby attraction that draws visitors, to whom you can offer accommodation.

Case Study

William bought his smallholding and quickly established a successful polytunnel and flock of poultry. He had a range

If you're lucky enough to have some spare buildings that you can convert, perhaps turn them into a B&B.

235

of buildings around the large yard that he used for storage. One day, someone asked if they could store their motorbikes and, looking into it, he found this was quite a good income. He cleared out his buildings, renovated them, installed a good security system and rented them out to owners of classic cars and motorbikes. He turned one building into a workshop. He still kept his growing interests, but was able to make good additional income from his storage.

How Much Can I Invest in a New Enterprise?

Adding value to a product usually requires investment. If you want to turn milk into cheese, fleeces into fibre or garments, you will need to invest. Most food processes will require not only planning permission but also meeting all the food regulations for hygiene and production. These can be daunting at first, but once broken down, are often just common sense. You may also need to invest in some equipment and perhaps even some part-time help.

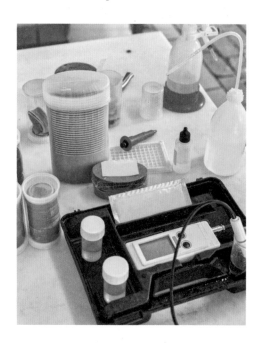

If you think you can make it work and you've done your sums, then be brave: there are plenty of small businesses that do well enough to provide a living. It will be very hard work and the hourly rate for the time you put in will initially be very low, but if you are prepared for this and the market is out there, then it is very rewarding.

Will My Family Help Me?

Let's be very clear: they don't have to actually make the cheese, change the beds in your farm bed and breakfast, or muck out the extra pigs. They do, however, have to be supportive. You can't make any new business work without devoting time and effort to it, so your partner will need to be on board so that he or she can make their contribution either by helping directly or by supporting your efforts. The same goes for children. Many young people appreciate being able to help out in a new business for the promise of some pocket money, and it gives them invaluable experience in the world of work (but watch out for the regulations on child employment!).

What Skills Do I Have And What Do I Need?

Time to do a skills assessment. Analysing professional skills such as education and training or practical skills such as fencing or building are easy. It's the hidden ones that you must also include. You've brought up four children? You are an expert in time management, organization, negotiating and education! You've got your old Land Rover on the road? You have significant machinery skills! On the parish council? You have insight into local government and politics. You organize an event for your local club? Administrative and personnel skills. Don't underestimate yourself.

Where you have gaps, identify them and look for courses to plug them. You can find many courses online and for free. You might have to invest some money in a bookkeeping course or a marketing course, but it will be money well spent. Practical skills normally need someone to show you how, so if you want to take your cheese making, jam making or spinning further, you will need to seek out an expert.

Case Study

Jane has managed the talks programme of her local club for some years. She's confident when dealing with a large group of people. She also loves sheep and spinning. Starting in a small way, she decided to use one of her buildings to teach spinning and now she gets in guest speakers in fibre who dye, spin and felt, and offers half-day and day courses. She is also much in demand as a speaker herself and is on the lists of various clubs. She also uses this as a way to promote her wool and crafts.

What Time Do I Have?

Again, honesty is needed here. There are only so many hours in a day, and only so many days that you can work without a break. If you are looking at going to markets, remember you have to get ready as well as attend, and then also unload and count up takings, process orders and answer queries. It's going to take more than one day, in reality.

Horses on the Holding

Does the horse, pony or donkey have a place in smallholding? Lots of smallholders think so and want to keep a horse for riding or driving for pleasure. Here are some points to consider when keeping horses, ponies or donkeys:

Available Space

If you move to the country with your own horses, remember that they will substantially reduce the grazing available to all other livestock. They will be a cost, not a benefit. To be truly self-sufficient, you don't need more than a couple of strong ponies for farm work, probably a mother and her offspring to bring on (rear).

Suitable Grazing

Although sheep and cattle eat some grass that horses don't touch, that doesn't mean that, when a horse has finished grazing, sheep or cattle can live only on the rough stuff left to them – mixed grazing is beneficial, as it breaks the worm cycle between species, but it also takes its toll on the grazing.

Compatibility

Equines and stock often don't mix. Cattle can eat tails of horses, horned animals can cause them damage, while horses can injure smaller livestock such as lambs. Donkeys can be aggressive to animals smaller than themselves.

239

Your Skills and Expertise

Working horses and ponies need thorough, knowledgeable training and a young animal can inadvertently be dangerous. Driving is particularly skillful and there is no such thing as a quiet breed of horse or pony. Years of work and training go into making a shire horse a working animal.

Type of Work

Decide what you want your working animal to do. Does it need to pull a cart of produce or logs? Do you want to work it in draught to cultivate land or to harrow a field? Or maybe you want to ride to inaccessible places to check on stock (as did shepherds of days gone past)? Match your needs

Top Tip

Some licks are toxic between species – check the label, especially for copper.

240

to a breed. For many purposes, a strong 14.2-hand pony will be more than sufficient, but if you are planning to haul large timber or plough clay ground, then you will need the strength of a draught horse.

Top Tip

Always have third-party insurance for your equines if riding or driving. In the UK, the British Horse Society and the British Driving Society offer insurance as part of their membership as well as a range of other benefits.

Donkey Power

A donkey isn't a long eared horse. Though part of the equine family, they are quite different animals and have their own traits and needs. Here's the low-down on donkeys:

▶ **Beasts of burden up to a point:** Donkeys can carry panniers for transporting goods, be used to 'drive to' a vehicle (that is, pull a carriage) and can work in draught pulling. Although strong, they should never carry a weight of more than 50 kg (8 st/110 lb).

▶ **Not as awkward as supposed:** They have less of a flight instinct than horses and tend to learn by repetition. Their stubborn reputation is undeserved; when they hesitate to do something, it is because they are not sure what you want or whether it is safe. Refusal to move is a training issue, not a natural trait.

▶ **Built for hot climes:** They originate from the desert and have different needs to a pony. Unlike the tough native pony with its thick winter waterproof coat, donkeys are not naturally waterproof and must always have man-made shelter.

▶ **Need company:** Never keep a donkey on its own (or a pony, for that matter); they need companions of their own kind.

Harness Up

There is an increasing interest in using smaller ponies and donkeys for working, and so equipment is becoming more widely available. The USA is leading the way at the moment, with contributions from people such as the Amish, who have always worked the land with equines, and it is opening up the ability to work a wider range of horses and ponies. It is very important that the harness is well fitted and of good quality.

Training

All training, whether it be natural horsemanship or more conventional methods, should work with the horse's, pony's or donkey's natural behaviour. If you are a novice, take lessons in driving or riding before buying an animal and continue with your lessons after purchase. If training, you will need to plan regular sessions that progress from leading to driving to pulling, making sure the horse, pony or donkey understands each step as you move to the next one. Bullying, shouting and using the whip have no place in basic training. Seek help from an expert if you cannot progress a step. Remember that a horse or donkey behaves and sees life as a horse or donkey, not as a human – they will work with you if you present the training in a form they can understand and accept.

Take Advice

There are many sanctuaries and organizations you can approach for advice and information. The UK's Donkey Sanctuary has a free-to-download manual on their website and over 30 advice sheets ranging from feeding to the costs of keeping. The Donkey Breed Society can provide advice on riding and driving and have events countrywide where you can learn more about the animal.

A Smallholding Way of Life

The ethos of smallholding extends into life as a whole. There seems no sense in spending time and effort growing your own in harmony with nature and then using unnecessary chemicals in your everyday life.

Keeping (Most) of the Dirt Outside

The old saying 'you have to eat a peck of dirt before you die' has some truth to it, in that exposing the body to low levels of bacteria results in the body developing its own resistance. (Slightly scarily, the 'peck' is equal to two gallons – that's a lot of dirt!) But the idea behind this is that you are aiming at a healthily clean house and surroundings, not a sterile environment. So you can expect a certain amount of dirt, but here are a couple of very simple measures to keep the outside outside:

▶ **Have a porch:** This acts as a crossover point between the mucky, muddy outside world and the kitchen. Take off your muddy boots and wash your hands. Have somewhere to put your outdoor clothing.

▶ **Have a curtain of strips or beads:** Although seemingly old-fashioned, this will reduce flies and dust from outside when you have the back door open.

243

Natural Cleaning Products

Nature's cleaning cupboard is well stocked if you know some of her secrets. Here are a few effective (and very cheap!) cleansers:

▶ **Lemon juice:** This contains naturally occurring citric acid. It is ideal for washing up due to the fact that it acts upon grease. It's also good for cleaning brass and copper. The juice can be extracted for use or you can simply cut a lemon in half and use it like that. Lime juice has similar properties.

▶ **Vinegar:** Vinegar, otherwise known as acetic acid, has been shown to act as a disinfectant and, like lemon and lime juice, it acts efficiently on grease. It also deodorizes. It can be used neat or diluted. White wine vinegar is similar, but is also good for carpet and fabric stains. You can use waste vinegar from pickles to clean the sink.

▶ **Bicarbonate of soda (baking soda):** Sodium bicarbonate is an effective and non-toxic all-rounder. It will remove stains in washing and can be used for washing up, cleaning a wide range of items from aluminium to porcelain and even silver.

▶ **Tea tree oil:** This is anti-bacterial and acts as a fungicide, but it is very safe to use within the home. It will kill mould, so is great for showers and bathrooms and has a lovely sharp smell.

▶ **Beeswax:** This has been a favourite of home cleaning since time immemorial. It is the basis of all the best polishes and can be used not only for shining but also for protecting. But a word of warning, if you are making your own polish by melting beeswax, it is highly flammable.

▶ **Herbs:** Bay, basil, lavender, lemon balm, peppermint, rosemary, thyme, sage and spearmint are just some of the herbs that are anti-bacterial and also antiseptic. What's more, they all smell wonderful. Basil, lavender, peppermint and thyme also act as disinfectants, fungicides and insect repellents. You can make an infusion to spray or hang dried bunches up in the kitchen or bathroom.

Be a Smallholder and Forager

Seasonal eating, foraging and hunting go hand in hand. The appearance of fresh young nettles means the opportunity for a new kind of green veg for the forager, but they won't last long, as they will grow coarser and become inedible. So these make a special spring treat. The autumn brings a cornucopia of nuts, fruits and fungi.

A Few Basic Rules

Top Tip

If you preserve anything and it does not smell fresh or shows signs of mould when you open it – discard and do not use.

▶ **Sustainability is key:** Never take everything; there must be enough left for natural restocking, whether it be fruit, fungi or even birds or animals. Always leave plenty for the wildlife who depend on the food for their survival.

▶ **Know the law:** There are well-enforced laws to protect many plants and animals and they are there to ensure their survival. Do not take anything covered by these laws.

▶ **Do not trespass:** The plants and animals in a wood or field will belong to the landowner. For picking such things as berries, the landowner will often give permission.

245

▶ **Be sure of your aim:** If you are shooting for the pot, make sure you can shoot without wounding, that you have permission to be there and that you take things that are permitted. If pigeon shooting, learn to recognize the various types, as some pigeons, such as rock doves, are now very scarce and turtle doves are under threat.

▶ **Be sure you can use all that you take:** Waste in foraging is particularly unforgivable, as some other species or human could have eaten it.

And finally, one of the most important rules:

▶ **Be sure you can identify what you are taking:** You must be absolutely sure that what you are taking is what you think it is. There have been incidents where people have mistaken poisonous for edible fungi with fatal results. If you are not sure, don't pick.

Foraging For Fruit

Among plants that make wonderful foraging are blackberries, elderflower, hawthorn, sloes and rosehips. All of these have one thing in common – they contain high levels of vitamin C, so jams, jellies and syrups all help you to keep well in the winter.

Waste Not Want Not

This is the smallholder's motto. Food waste is unforgivable on any level and smallholders are particularly adept at being prudent with food from production to consumption. Careful preserving will help cope with excesses of crops, and swapping with other smallholders and growers will provide variety whilst using up gluts.

Checklist

▶ **Land at a cost:** Land prices vary according to location and desirability; don't expect to pay basic agricultural land prices.

▶ **Add value to your smallholding:** Make something extra special out of your produce or use your smallholding's unique features.

▶ **Money, time and a plan:** These are all essential for expansion ideas. Write a business plan and be accurate with the costs.

▶ **Identify your skills:** Evaluate your business skills and include life skills too.

▶ **Horses:** Horses can be a costly addition to the smallholding, so allow for this or think about them as a working animal.

▶ **Know the difference:** Donkeys are not small horses with long ears; they are different animals with their own needs and characteristics.

▶ **The natural way:** Carry on the smallholding ethos in the house with natural cleaning methods.

▶ **Wise foraging and economy in all:** Be a forager and a smallholder, but never take more than you need. Fight a war on food waste.

The Smallholding Year

There is much to do throughout the year on your smallholding. Here is a checklist of some key seasonal tasks.

Winter

▶ **Prepare the land for next year:** Digging, manuring, planning green manures.

▶ **Cut hedges:** Do this between September and February so as not to disturb nesting birds.

▶ **Plant hedges and trees:** This gives them a long time to get their roots established in the soil.

▶ **For sheep:** Put the ram in approximately five months before you want lambs; so for March, this would be October.

▶ **For goats:** Arrange the mating five months before kids are wanted.

Spring

▶ **Plan sowing and rotations:** Make sure first frosts have passed.

▶ **Supplements:** Feed pregnant ewes additional concentrates.

▶ **Egg time:** Collect eggs regularly from laying poultry.

▶ **For chicks:** Artificial incubation of eggs.

▶ **For lambs:** Bring sheep closer to home for lambing.

▶ **Sheep health:** Ensure sheep vaccinations are up to date.

▶ **Worming:** Worm livestock and/or do worm counts (if applicable; not all types of worms will show on a worm count).

Summer

▶ **Nutrition for milk:** Keep checking there is sufficient grass for lactating stock. If not, supplement the feed or change paddocks.

▶ **Check udders:** Also check lactating stock for mastitis.

▶ **Haymaking:** Take the opportunity to make hay when the weather permits.

▶ **Fly strike:** Use a preventative on sheep for fly strike; it may appear earlier than summer, so watch out for warm humid weather from spring onwards.

▶ **Shearing:** Get sheep and alpacas sheared.

▶ **Look after crops:** Keep vegetables weeded and watered, and start picking some crops.

▶ **Sow summer crops:** Such as successional sowings of salads.

▶ **Save soft fruit:** Freeze soft fruit for later use.

Autumn

▶ **Weaning:** If well grown, wean young stock from their mothers.

▶ **For meat:** Check all fattening stock for weight gain and give extra feed if necessary. Cull surplus cockerels and drakes for the freezer.

▶ **Nutrition for moulting:** Consider a vitamin supplement for hens in moult.

▶ **Harvest fruit:** Check orchard fruits and pick as they ripen.

▶ **Late crops:** Clear the veg patch and put in additional crops for winter, such as garlic and winter salads.

▶ **Preserve fruit and veg:** Make preserves and pickles.

▶ **Forage:** Nuts, fruits and fungi should be pentiful.

Further Reading

Abbott, Jez, *Allotment Gardening*, Flame Tree Publishing, 2010

Benard, Michael, *Homesteading 101 Handbook for Beginners*, CreateSpace Independent Publishing Platform, 2016

Buckingham, Alan, *Allotment Month by Month: How to Grow Your Own Fruit and Veg*, DK, 2009

Cornish, Sophie and Tucker, Holly, *Build a Business From Your Kitchen Table*, Simon & Schuster, 2012

Damerow, Gail, *Barnyard in Your Backyard: A Beginner's Guide to Raising Chickens, Ducks, Geese, Rabbits, Goats, Sheep and Cows*, Storey Publishing, 2002

Dawson, Simon, *The Self-Sufficiency Bible*, Watkins Publishing, 2013

Eales, Andrew; Small, John; and Macaldowie, Colin, *Practical Lambing and Lamb Care: A Veterinary Guide* (3rd Edition), Wiley-Blackwell, 2004

Emery, Carla, *The Encyclopedia of Country Living* (40th Anniversary Edition), Sasquatch Books, 2012

Fields, Harry, *Alpaca Keeping*, World Ideas, 2014

Gregory, Pam and Waring, Claire, *Keeping Bees*, Flame Tree Publishing, 2017

Jones, Steven, *Homesteading from Scratch: Building Your Self-Sufficient Homestead, Start to Finish*, Skyhorse Publishing, 2017

Morgan, Sally, *Living on One Acre or Less: How to Produce All the Fruit, Veg, Meat, Fish and Eggs Your Family Needs*, Green Books, 2016

Shankland, Liz, *Pig Manual: The Complete Step-by-Step Guide to Keeping Pigs,* J H Haynes and Co, 2016

Shankland, Liz, *Sheep Manual: The Complete Step-by-Step Guide to Keeping Sheep*, J H Haynes and Co, 2015

Shankland, Liz, *Smallholding Manual: The Complete Step-by-Step Guide to Smallholding*, J H Haynes and Co, 2012

Strauss, Rachelle, *Grow Your Own Vegetables,* Flame Tree Publishing, 2014

Smith, Cheryl K., *Raising Goats for Dummies*, John Wiley and Sons, 2010

Wright, Liz, *Keeping Chickens*, Flame Tree Publishing, 2017

Wright, Liz (Ed.), *Practical Poultry* magazine, Kelsey Media

Wright, Liz (Ed.), *Smallholding* magazine (previously *Practical Sheep, Goats & Alpacas*), Kelsey Media

Wyatt, Carson, *Raising Dairy Cattle for Beginners: A Simple Guide to Dairy Cattle for Milk and Eventually Meat*, CreateSpace Independent Publishing Platform, 2017

Wyatt, Carson, *Raising Ducks for Beginners Guide*, CreateSpace Independent Publishing Platform, 2017

Young, Rosamund, *The Secret Life of Cows*, Faber & Faber, 2017

Websites

www.accidentalsmallholder.net
Supplies information on smallholding and contains a forum to discuss experiences with others.

www.allotment-garden.org
Originally an online allotment growing diary, this website offers articles and advice, a chat and help forum, recipes and a shop for all your allotment gardening supplies.

www.beesbros.com
Step-by-step guide on how to keep bees and how to extract honey to use as an ingredient in recipes.

www.countrysmallholding.com
A website designed to help those getting started. It provides plentiful knowledge on livestock, land, poultry and equipment.

www.thedonkeysanctuary.org.uk
All you need to know about looking after donkeys. You can also download their Donkey Care Handbook here.

www.farminmypocket.co.uk
Offers information on home brew, livestock and gardening with a blog dedicated to providing a humorous insight to life as a smallholder.

www.fwi.co.uk
Farmer's weekly website showcasing new machinery and equipment as well as how-to guides, farming news and lots more.

www.groweatgather.co.uk
Information on welfare requirements for livestock being bred for slaughter.

www.homefarmer.co.uk
Offers guides and advice on being self-sufficient as well as suggesting DIY projects to get the most from your land.

www.homesteadingtoday.com
Forums with discussions on several topics across homesteading, including specific guidance on raising livestock.

www.poultrykeeper.com
Advice and guidance on how to keep turkeys, chickens, ducks, geese, quail and guinea fowl.

www.self-sufficient.co.uk
Articles on everything relating to smallholdings, including properties, recipes and livestock care.

www.smallholder.co.uk
Offering the latest news for smallholders with expert advice on raising livestock, showcasing them at competitions and how to get the best from your produce.

www.smalltownhomestead.com
Podcasts discussing gardening, livestock, food preservation, foraging, hunting, fishing and the know-how and skills of self-sufficient living.

www.suppliesforsmallholders.co.uk
An online shop offering advice for new smallholders along with delivering the best-quality supplies needed to be self-sufficient.

www.thriftyhomesteader.com
A guide to self-reliant living with blogs including recipes and advice on animal care.

www.viableselfsufficiency.co.uk
Contains forums and expert advice on getting started with fun activities for new smallholders to get involved in.

Index